William Shakespeare

Two Noble Kinsmen
In Plain and Simple English

BookCaps Study Guides
www.SwipeSpeare.com

© 2015. All Rights Reserved.

Table of Contents:

ABOUT THIS SERIES...3

COMPARATIVE VERSION 6

Prologue 7
Act I 8
    Scene I 9
    Scene II 19
    Scene III 24
    Scene IV 28
    Scene V 31
Act II 32
    Scene I 33
    Scene II 36
    Scene III 50
    Scene IV 55
    Scene V 57
    Scene VI 61
Act III 63
    Scene I 64
    Scene II 69
    Scene III 71
    Scene IV 76
    Scene V 78
    Scene VI 86
Act IV 120
    Scene I 121
    Scene II 128
    Scene III 137
    Scene IV 144

About This Series

The "Classic Retold" series started as a way of telling classics for the modern reader—being careful to preserve the themes and integrity of the original. Whether you want to understand Shakespeare a little more or are trying to get a better grasps of the Greek classics, there is a book waiting for you!

Characters

Hymen

Theseus

Hippolita

Bride to TheseusEmelia

Sister to Theseus[Emelia's Woman]

Nymphs

Three Queens

Three valiant Knights

Palamon, andArcite

The two Noble Kinsmen, in love with fair Emelia[Valerius]

Perithous,[A Herald]

[A Gentleman]

[A Messenger]

[A Servant]

[Wooer]

[Keeper]

Jaylor

His Daughter, in love with Palamon[His brother]

[A Doctor]

[4] Countreymen

[2 Friends of the Jaylor]

[3 Knights]

[Nel, and other]Wenches

A Taborer,Gerrold

A Schoolmaster.

Comparative Version

Prologue

(Prologue)

	Flourish.

New plays and maidenheads are near akin—
Much follow'd both, for both much money
gi'n,
If they stand sound and well; and a good play
(Whose modest scenes blush on his marriage-
day,
And shake to lose his honor) is like her
That after holy tie and first night's stir,
Yet still is modesty, and still retains
More of the maid to sight than husband's pains.
We pray our play may be so; for I am sure
It has a noble breeder and a pure,
A learned, and a poet never went
More famous yet 'twixt Po and silver Trent.
Chaucer (of all admir'd) the story gives;
There constant to eternity it lives.
If we let fall the nobleness of this,
And the first sound this child hear be a hiss,
How will it shake the bones of that good man,
And make him cry from under ground, "O, fan
From me the witless chaff of such a writer
That blasts my bays and my fam'd works
makes lighter
Than Robin Hood!" This is the fear we bring;
For to say truth, it were an endless thing,
And too ambitious, to aspire to him,
Weak as we are, and almost breathless swim
In this deep water. Do but you hold out
Your helping hands, and we shall tack about
And something do to save us. You shall hear
Scenes, though below his art, may yet appear
Worth two hours' travail. To his bones sweet
sleep!
Content to you! If this play do not keep
A little dull time from us, we perceive
Our losses fall so thick we must needs leave.

New plays and virginity are very alike–
both much chased after, both given for a high
price,
if they are genuine; and a good play
(whose modest scenes blush on its first time,
and shake at losing its honour) is like her
who after the marriage and the first night's
activity, remains modest and looks
more like a maid than one who's been with a
husband. We pray our play may be like this; for
I am sure it has a noble ancestor, pure,
learned, there was never a more famous poet
between the River Po and the silver Trent.
Chaucer, admired by everyone, wrote the plot;
and so it lives in eternity.
If we fall from this high standard,
and the first sound this child hears is a hiss,
how it will shake the bones of that good man,
and make him cry from underground, "Oh
separate me from the drivel of such a writer
who is destroying my fame and making my
great works
seem lighter than Robin Hood!" This is what
worries us; to tell the truth, it would take
forever, and would be too ambitious, to hope to
be like him, weak as we are, we are almost
breathless swimming
in this deep water. Just hold out
your helping hands, and we shall turn around
and try and save ourselves. You shall hear
scenes that, although not as great as his, might
still seem worth a couple of hours' watching.
May he rest in peace!
May you be happy! If this play doesn't stave off
boredom for a while, we can see
we will suffer such losses that we must give up.

Flourish.

Act I

Scene I

Athens. Before a temple.

(Hymen, Boy, Nymphs, Theseus, Hippolyta, Pirithous, Emilia, Artesius, Attendants, Three Queens)

Enter Hymen with a torch burning; a Boy, in a white robe, before, singing and strewing flow'rs; after Hymen, a Nymph, encompass'd in her tresses, bearing a wheaten garland; then Theseus, between two other Nymphs with wheaten chaplets an their heads; then Hippolyta, the bride, led by Pirithous, and another holding a garland over her head (her tresses likewise hanging; after her, Emilia, holding up her train; Artesius and Attendants.

BOY
Roses, their sharp spines being gone,
Not royal in their smells alone,
But in their hue;
Maiden pinks, of odor faint,
Daisies smell-less, yet most quaint,
And sweet thyme true;
Primrose, first-born child of Ver,
Merry spring-time's harbinger,
With her bells dim;
Oxlips in their cradles growing,
Marigolds on death-beds blowing,
Larks'-heels trim;
All dear Nature's children sweet,
Lie 'fore bride and bridegroom's feet.
Strew flowers.
Blessing their sense;
Not an angel of the air,
Bird melodious, or bird fair,
Is absent hence.
The crow, the sland'rous cuckoo, nor
The boding raven, nor chough hoar,
Nor chatt'ring pie,
May on our bridehouse perch or sing,
Or with them any discord bring,
But from it fly.

Music. The Song by the Boy.
Roses, once their thorns are gone,
are not made royal only by their perfume,
but by their colour as well;
maiden pinks which smell little,
daisies which don't smell but are pretty,
and true sweet thyme;
primroses, first flower of spring,
signalling the happy start of springtime
with her muted bells;
oxlips growing in their cradles,
marigolds blowing over graves,
neat larks'-heels;
all of dear Nature's sweet children
are lying at the bride and bridegroom's feet.
They bless their senses;
not one angel of the air,
sweet singing or beautiful bird,
is missing.
The crow, the lying cuckoo,
the ominous raven, the cold cough,
nor the chattering magpie,
may not sit on the wedding house or sing
or bring any discord here,
they should fly away.

Enter three Queens, in black, with veils stain'd, with imperial crowns. The first Queen falls down at the foot of Theseus; the second falls down at the foot of Hippolyta; the third before Emilia.

9

FIRST QUEEN.
For pity's sake and true gentility's,
Hear and respect me.

For the sake of pity and nobility,
hear me and respect me.

SECOND QUEEN.
For your mother's sake,
And as you wish your womb may thrive with
fair ones,
Hear and respect me.

For the sake of your mother,
and your future hopes of beautiful children,
hear me and respect me.

THIRD QUEEN.
Now for the love of him whom Jove hath
mark'd
The honor of your bed, and for the sake
Of clear virginity, be advocate
For us and our distresses! This good deed
Shall raze you out o' th' book of trespasses
All you are set down there.

Now for the love of the one whom Jove has
chosen
to honour your bed, and in the name
of pure virginity, speak out
for us and our misfortunes! This good deed
will wipe out all your sins.

THESEUS
Sad lady, rise.

Sad lady, get up.

HIPPOLYTA
Stand up.

Stand up.

EMILIA
No knees to me.
What woman I may stead that is distress'd
Does bind me to her.

There's no need to kneel to me.
If a woman is in trouble and needs my help
I will not fail her.

THESEUS
What's your request? Deliver you for all.

What do you want to ask for? You speak for all
of you.

FIRST QUEEN.
We are three queens, whose sovereigns fell
before
The wrath of cruel Creon; who endured
The beaks of ravens, talents of the kites,
And pecks of crows in the foul fields of
Thebes.
He will not suffer us to bum their bones,
To urn their ashes, nor to take th' offense
Of mortal loathsomeness from the blest eye
Of holy Phoebus, but infects the winds
With stench of our slain lords. O, pity, Duke,
Thou purger of the earth, draw thy fear'd sword

We are three queens, whose husbands were
killed by the anger of cruel Creon; their bodies
were torn by the beaks of ravens, the claws of
kites, and the pecking of crows in the foul fields
of Thebes. He won't let us cremate them,
to put their ashes in an urn, or to take the
horrible sight of rotting corpses away from the
blessed sight of the holy sun, but lets the stench
of our dead husbands reek through the air.
Pity us, Duke, you who has cleaned the earth,
draw your fearsome sword

That does good turns to th' world; give us the bones
Of our dead kings, that we may chapel them;
And of thy boundless goodness take some note
That for our crowned heads we have no roof,
Save this which is the lion's, and the bear's,
And vault to every thing!

THESEUS
Pray you kneel not;
I was transported with your speech, and suffer'd
Your knees to wrong themselves. I have heard the fortunes
Of your dead lords, which gives me such lamenting
As wakes my vengeance and revenge for 'em.
King Capaneus was your lord. The day
That he should marry you, at such a season
As now it is with me, I met your groom
By Mars's altar. You were that time fair;
Not Juno's mantle fairer than your tresses,
Nor in more bounty spread her. Your wheaten wreath
Was then nor thresh'd nor blasted; Fortune at you
Dimpled her cheek with smiles. Hercules our kinsman
(Then weaker than your eyes) laid by his club;
He tumbled down upon his Nemean hide,
And swore his sinews thaw'd. O grief and time,
Fearful consumers, you will all devour!

FIRST QUEEN.
O, I hope some god,
Some god hath put his mercy in your manhood,
Whereto he'll infuse pow'r, and press you forth
Our undertaker.

THESEUS
O, no knees, none, widow!
Unto the helmeted Bellona use them,
And pray for me your soldier.
Troubled I am.

SECOND QUEEN.

that does good deeds for the world; get the bones of our dead kings for us so we can have a proper funeral; and in your infinite goodness please note that we have no roof over our royal heads, apart from this sky which we share with the lion, the bear and everything!

Please don't kneel; I was absorbed in what you said, and wrongly allowed you to stay on your knees. I have heard about the fates of your dead husbands, and it makes me so sad that it inspires me to take revenge for them. Your husband was King Capaneus. On your wedding day, on the same occasion I am now enjoying, I met your groom at the altar of Mars. You were lovely at that time; Juno's cloak was not more lovely than your hair, nor more plentiful. Your golden locks hadn't been torn or windblown; Fortune smiled upon you. Our kinsman Hercules (who then had less power than your eyes) put down his club; he tumbled down on his Nemean hide, and swore he had become weak. Oh grief and time, with your terrible greed, you will devour everything!

Oh, I hope some god has added mercy to your manly virtues, which he will make work and employ you to do this service for us.

Oh, no kneeling, widow! Use your knees to pray to the goddess of war, and pray for me as your soldier. I am troubled. Turns away.

Honored Hippolyta,
Most dreaded Amazonian, that hast slain
The scythe-tusk'd boar; that with thy arm, as strong
As it is white, wast near to make the male
To thy sex captive, but that this thy lord,
Born to uphold creation in that honor
First Nature styl'd it in, shrunk thee into
The bound thou wast o'erflowing, at once subduing
Thy force and thy affection; soldieress
That equally canst poise sternness with pity,
Whom now I know hast much more power on him
Than ever he had on thee, who ow'st his strength,
And his love too, who is a servant for
The tenor of thy speech; dear glass of ladies,
Bid him that we, whom flaming war doth scorch,
Under the shadow of his sword may cool us;
Require him he advance it o'er our heads;
Speak't in a woman's key—like such a woman
As any of us three; weep ere you fail;
Lend us a knee;
But touch the ground for us no longer time
Than a dove's motion when the head's pluck'd off;
Tell him, if he i' th' blood-siz'd field lay swoll'n,
Showing the sun his teeth, grinning at the moon,
What you would do.

Respected Hippolyta,
Most feared Amazonian, who has killed
the sharp-tusked boar; you who almost,
with your strong white arm, subdued
the male sex, until your lord here,
this perfect specimen
of Nature, pushed your advances
back, capturing your force and your love;
as a soldier you can show both sternness and pity,
and I now know you have much more power over him
than he ever had over you, you have captured his force
and his love too, he will do
anything you say; dear perfect lady,
tell him that we, burned by flaming war,
want to be cooled in the shade of his sword;
tell him to hold it over our heads;
speak to him as a woman - a woman like any of us;
weep before you admit defeat;
kneel to him;
but don't do so for longer
than a dove keeps moving when its head is cut off;
tell him what you would do if he lay rotting
on a blood-soaked battlefield, turning into a skeleton
beneath the open skies.

HIPPOLYTA

Poor lady, say no more:
I had as lief trace this good action with you
As that whereto I am going, and never yet
Went I so willing way. My lord is taken
Heart-deep with your distress. Let him consider.
I'll speak anon.

Poor lady, say no more:
I'm as happy to help you
as I am to be married, and I was never
happier about anything than that. My lord
feels your distress deep in his heart. Let him think.
I'll speak to him soon.

THIRD QUEEN.

O, my petition was
Set down in ice, which by hot grief uncandied

Kneel to Emilia.
Oh, my request was

Set down in ice, which by hot grief uncandied
Melts into drops; so sorrow wanting form
Is press'd with deeper matter.

EMILIA
Pray stand up,
Your grief is written in your cheek.

THIRD QUEEN.
O, woe,
You cannot read it there. There, through my tears,
Like wrinkled pebbles in a glassy stream,
You may behold 'em. Lady, lady, alack!
He that will all the treasure know o' th' earth
Must know the centre too; he that will fish
For my least minnow, let him lead his line
To catch one at my heart. O, pardon me,
Extremity, that sharpens sundry wits,
Makes me a fool.

EMILIA
Pray you say nothing, pray you.
Who cannot feel nor see the rain, being in't,
Knows neither wet nor dry. If that you were
The ground-piece of some painter, I would buy you
T' instruct me 'gainst a capital grief indeed—
Such heart-pierc'd demonstration! But alas,
Being a natural sister of our sex,
Your sorrow beats so ardently upon me
That it shall make a counter-reflect 'gainst
My brother's heart, and warm it to some pity,
Though it were made of stone. Pray have good comfort.

THESEUS
Forward to th' temple. Leave not out a jot
O' th' sacred ceremony.

FIRST QUEEN.
O, this celebration
Will long last and be more costly than
Your suppliants' war! Remember that your fame

*written on ice, which was melted by
bitter hot grief; so sorrow cannot show itself
when faced with such a great evil.*

*Please stand up,
your grief is obvious from your face.*

*Oh, you cannot see my sorrow there. You can
see my cheeks under my tears like wrinkled
pebbles in a watery stream.
Alas, lady! Someone who wants the treasure of
the earth must dig into it; if you want to know
any part of my grief
you have to look deep into my heart. Oh,
pardon me, extreme suffering, that makes some
people sharper,
makes me a fool.*

*Please, I beg you, say nothing.
Someone who can't see or feel the rain,
when they're in it,
knows nothing. If you were
a painting, I would buy you
to keep as an example of the greatest sorrow-
such a heartrending example! But alas,
as all we women are sisters,
your sorrow affects me so deeply
that it will reflect off me into
my brother's heart, and kindle pity there
even if it were made of stone. Please be sure of
that.*

*Onward to the temple. Don't leave out a word
of the sacred ceremony.*

*Oh, this celebration
will last a long time and cost more
than the war we have been in! Remember that
you*

Knolls in the ear o' th' world; what you do quickly
Is not done rashly; your first thought is more
Than others' labored meditance; your premeditating
More than their actions. But, O Jove, your actions,
Soon as they move, as asprays do the fish,
Subdue before they touch. Think, dear Duke, think
What beds our slain kings have!

are famous throughout the world; what you do quickly is not done hotheadedly; your initial thought is worth more than the long contemplation of others; your plans are worth more than their actions. But, by god, once you start moving your actions subdue men before they even begin, as the shadow of the osprey scares the fish. Think, dear Duke, think of where our dead kings are lying!

SECOND QUEEN.
What griefs our beds
That our dear lords have none!

How sad we are in our beds, knowing our dear lords have none!

THIRD QUEEN.
None fit for th' dead:
Those that with cords, knives, drams, precipitance,
Weary of this world's light, have to themselves
Been death's most horrid agents, humane grace
Affords them dust and shadow.

None that are fit for the dead: those who have brought death upon themselves, tired of living, in the most horrible ways, with hanging, stabbing, poison, leaping from heights, the kindness of humanity allows them a decent burial.

FIRST QUEEN.
But our lords
Lie blist'ring 'fore the visitating sun,
And were good kings when living.

But our lords are lying burning under the hot sun, and they were good kings when they were alive.

THESEUS
It is true; and I will give you comfort
To give your dead lords graves; the which to do
Must make some work with Creon.

It is true; and I will bring you peace by making sure your dead lords are buried; to do this I'll have to take on Creon.

FIRST QUEEN.
And that work presents itself to th' doing:
Now 'twill take form, the heats are gone tomorrow.
Then, bootless toil must recompense itself
With its own sweat; now he's secure,
Not dreams we stand before your puissance
Wrinching our holy begging in our eyes
To make petition clear.

And the best chance of success is to do it now: strike while the iron's hot. Tomorrow, fruitless work will only bring sweat; at the moment he thinks he's safe, and doesn't dream we are standing before your majesty, weeping as we explain the holy task we want you to perform.

SECOND QUEEN.
Now you may take him

Now you could beat him,

Drunk with his victory.

THIRD QUEEN.
And his army full
Of bread and sloth.

THESEUS
Artesius, that best knowest
How to draw out, fit to this enterprise,
The prim'st for this proceeding, and the number
To carry such a business, forth and levy
Our worthiest instruments, whilst we dispatch
This grand act of our life, this daring deed
Of fate in wedlock.

FIRST QUEEN.
Dowagers, take hands,
Let us be widows to our woes; delay
Commends us to a famishing hope.

ALL QUEENS.
Farewell.

SECOND QUEEN.
We come unseasonably; but when could grief
Cull forth, as unpang'd judgment can, fitt'st time
For best solicitation?

THESEUS
Why, good ladies,
This is a service, whereto I am going,
Greater than any war; it more imports me
Than all the actions that I have foregone,
Or futurely can cope.

FIRST QUEEN.
The more proclaiming
Our suit shall be neglected. When her arms,
Able to lock Jove from a synod, shall
By warranting moonlight corslet thee—O, when
Her twinning cherries shall their sweetness fall
Upon thy tasteful lips, what wilt thou think
Of rotten kings or blubber'd queens? What care
For what thou feel'st not? What thou feel'st

while he's drunk with celebrating victory.

*And his army
are stuffed and lazy.*

*Artesius, you know best
how to choose the best men for this business,
and what numbers we will need
to carry it out; go out and raise
our finest soldiers, while I finish
this great act of my life, this brave
act of committing to marriage.*

*Dowagers, join hands.
Let us go on with our mourning;
delay starves our hopes.*

Farewell.

*We have come at a bad time, but how can grief
choose, as emotionless judgement can, the best time
to put itself forward?*

*Why, good ladies, the business I am
undertaking now is greater than any war; it's
more important to me than anything I've ever done,
or will do.*

*This tells us
our requests will not be answered. When her arms,
which could keep Jove from a meeting, are
wrapped round you in the sweet moonlight -
oh, when her cherry red lips give their
sweetness to yours, what thought will you give
to rotting kings or weeping queens? What will you*

being able
To make Mars spurn his drum. O, if thou couch
But one night with her, every hour in't will
Take hostage of thee for a hundred, and
Thou shalt remember nothing more than what
That banquet bids thee to!

care about things you can't feel? What you'll be feeling would be enough to make Mars give up war. Oh, if you sleep just one night with her, every hour of it will make you stay for a hundred more, and you'll be thinking of nothing but the feast you're enjoying there!

HIPPOLYTA
Though much unlike
You should be so transported, as much sorry
I should be such a suitor; yet I think
Did I not by th' abstaining of my joy,
Which breeds a deeper longing, cure their surfeit
That craves a present med'cine, I should pluck
All ladies' scandal on me. Therefore, sir,
Kneels.
As I shall here make trial of my pray'rs,
Either presuming them to have some force,
Or sentencing for aye their vigor dumb,
Prorogue this business we are going about, and hang
Your shield afore your heart, about that neck
Which is my fee, and which I freely lend
To do these poor queens service.

Though it's very unlikely that you would forget your duty like this, I would be very sorry to be the cause of it; but I think that if I didn't hold back from my pleasure, which can only make desire stronger, to cure their illness which needs medicine at once, all women would be horrified with me. Therefore, sir, [kneels] I shall now test what value my pleas have, either thinking that they have some influence, or letting me know never to ask again, I ask you to postpone our current business, and place your shield in front of your heart, round the neck which belongs to me, and which I freely lend to help these poor queens.

ALL QUEENS
O, help now!
Our cause cries for your knee.

To Emilia.
Oh, help us now!
Our cause needs you to plead for us.

EMILIA
If you grant not
My sister her petition, in that force,
With that celerity and nature, which
She makes it in, from henceforth I'll not dare
To ask you any thing, nor be so hardy
Ever to take a husband.

Kneels.
If you do not give my sister what she's asking for, with the same strength, speed and spirit with which she's asking, from now on I won't dare ask you for anything, or be so foolish as to ever get married.

THESEUS
Pray stand up.

Please stand up.

I am entreating of myself to do
That which you kneel to have me. Pirithous,
Lead on the bride; get you and pray the gods
For success and return; omit not any thing
In the pretended celebration. Queens,

I am pleading with myself to do the thing which you are begging me. Pirithous, you lead the bride; go and pray to the gods for our success and safe return; don't omit any element of our intended celebration.

Follow your soldier.
To Artesius.
As before, hence you,
And at the banks of Aulis meet us with
The forces you can raise, where we shall find
The moi'ty of a number for a business
More bigger-look'd.

Exit Artesius.

To Hippolyta.
Since that our theme is haste,
I stamp this kiss upon thy currant lip.
Sweet, keep it as my token. Set you forward,
For I will see you gone.

Exeunt slowly towards the temple.

Farewell, my beauteous sister. Pirithous,
Keep the feast full, bate not an hour on't.

PIRITHOUS
Sir,
I'll follow you at heels; the feast's solemnity
Shall want till your return.

THESEUS
Cousin, I charge you
Boudge not from Athens. We shall be returning
Ere you can end this feast, of which I pray you
Make no abatement. Once more, farewell all.

FIRST QUEEN.
Thus dost thou still make good
The tongue o' th' world.

SECOND QUEEN.
And earn'st a deity
Equal with Mars.

THIRD QUEEN.
If not above him, for
Thou being but mortal makest affections bend
To godlike honors; they themselves, some say,
Groan under such a mast'ry.

Queens, follow me.
[To Artesius]
As we've done before, you go,
and meet me at the banks of the Aulis with
what forces you can gather, while I shall gather
another group for a business
that's bigger than it looks.

[To Hippolyta]
Since we have to hurry,
I kiss your true lips.
Darling, keep this as a symbol of my love. Get
going, I want to see you go.

Farewell, my beautiful sister. Pirithous,
follow all the plans for the celebrations, don't
cut it short by an hour.

Sir,
I'll follow you; the celebration of the feast
can wait until you return.

Cousin, I order you
not to move from Athens. We shall be coming
back before the end of this feast, which I'm
asking you
not to cut short. Once more, farewell to all.

So you live up to
your reputation.

And make yourself a god,
equal to Mars.

If not greater than him, for
being just a mortal that makes the mind
offer you the honours due to gods; some say the
gods could not bear such tasks as you do.

THESEUS
As we are men
Thus should we do, being sensually subdu'd
We lose our human title. Good cheer, ladies.
Now turn we towards your comforts.

This is what we should do,
being men, if we lose our sympathy
we stop being human. Be in good spirits,
ladies. We're now coming to your aid.

Flourish. Exeunt.

Scene II

Thebes. The palace.

(Palamon, Arcite, Valerius)

Enter Palamon and Arcite.

ARCITE

Dear Palamon, dearer in love than blood,
And our prime cousin, yet unhard'ned in
The crimes of nature—let us leave the city
Thebes, and the temptings in't, before we
further
Sully our gloss of youth:
And here to keep in abstinence we shame
As in incontinence; for not to swim
I' th' aid o' th' current were almost to sink,
At least to frustrate striving, and to follow
The common stream, 'twould bring us to an
eddy
Where we should turn or drown; if labor
through,
Our gain but life and weakness.

PALAMON
Your advice
Is cried up with example. What strange ruins,
Since first we went to school, may we perceive
Walking in Thebes! Scars and bare weeds
The gain o' th' martialist, who did propound
To his bold ends honor and golden ingots,
Which though he won, he had not; and now
flurted
By peace, for whom he fought, who then shall
offer
To Mars's so scorn'd altar? I do bleed
When such I meet, and wish great Juno would
Resume her ancient fit of jealousy
To get the soldier work, that peace might purge
For her repletion, and retain anew

Her charitable heart, now hard, and harsher
Than strife or war could be.

Dear Palamon, whom I love more than kinship demands,
my first cousin, still
an innocent—let's leave the city
of Thebes, and its temptations, before we
corrupt our youthful virtues further;
to maintain our abstinence is seen, here,
as being as shameful as indulgence; to swim
against the tide would almost drown us,
or at least stop us struggling and go
with the common flow, which would bring us to
a whirlpool
where we would have to change or drown; if we
got through,
all we would gain would be life and illness.

Your advice is supported by examples. What
terrible hardship we have seen walking around
Thebes, since we first came here to school!
Scars and ragged clothes are the rewards of the
soldier, who fought boldly for honour and for
gold, which, although he won them, he didn't
get to keep; and now he is an outcast in the
time of peace for which he fought, who would
bother being a soldier? It wounds me when I
meet people like that, and makes me wish great
Juno would start another war to get the soldier
work, that peace would purge herself
and regain her
charitable heart, which is now hard, and
harsher
than any war or fighting could be.

ARCITE

Are you not out?
Meet you no ruin but the soldier in
The cranks and turns of Thebes? You did begin
As if you met decays of many kinds.
Perceive you none that do arouse your pity
But th' unconsider'd soldier?

PALAMON

Yes, I pity
Decays where e'er I find them, but such most
That sweating in an honorable toil
Are paid with ice to cool 'em.

ARCITE

'Tis not this
I did begin to speak of. This is virtue
Of no respect in Thebes. I spake of Thebes,
How dangerous, if we will keep our honors,
It is for our residing; where every evil
Hath a good color; where ev'ry seeming good's
A certain evil; where not to be ev'n jump
As they are, here were to be strangers, and
Such things to be, mere monsters.

PALAMON

'Tis in our power
(Unless we fear that apes can tutor's) to
Be masters of our manners. What need I
Affect another's gait, which is not catching
Where there is faith? Or to be fond upon
Another's way of speech, when by mine own
I may be reasonably conceiv'd; sav'd too,
Speaking it truly? Why am I bound
By any generous bond to follow him
Follows his tailor, haply so long until
The follow'd make pursuit? Or let me know
Why mine own barber is unblest, with him
My poor chin too, for 'tis not scissor'd just
To such a favorite's glass? What canon is there
That does command my rapier from my hip,
To dangle't in my hand, or to go tiptoe
Before the street be foul? Either I am
The forehorse in the team, or I am none
That draw i' th' sequent trace. These poor slight
sores

Aren't you missing something?
Do you meet no ruined people but soldiers in
the pathways and alleys of Thebes? You started
as if you met many different types of ruined
people. Do you see nobody that inspires pity in
you apart from the neglected soldier?

Yes, I pity
the downfallen wherever I find them, but
particularly those that have done honourable
service and are rejected once it's done.

That's not what
I was going to talk about. This sort of thing
is not unique to Thebes. I was speaking of
how dangerous it will be to stay in Thebes,
if we want to keep our honour; everything evil
is well thought of; everything that seems good
is bound to be evil; and not to follow what
others do makes us foreigners, and
as such we will be despised.

We are quite capable
(unless we are worried that we will stop
copying apes)
of keeping control of ourselves. Why should I
copy someone else's way of walking, it won't
affect me if I have faith. Why would I copy
someone else's speech, when my own is
perfectly good for getting my meaning across;
better, because it's genuine? Why should I have
to consider myself bound to follow someone
who follows his tailor, maybe for so long that
he'll turn round and chase him off? Tell me
what's wrong with my own barber, what's
wrong with my poor chin, just because my
beard isn't cut in imitation of some favourite?
What law is there that says I should take my
rapier from my hip, carrying it in my hand, or
that I should walk on tiptoes before the street is
mucky? I must either be a leader or nothing, I
will not be a follower. These minor injuries

Need not a plantin; that which rips my bosom
Almost to th' heart's—

ARCITE
Our uncle Creon.

PALAMON
He,
A most unbounded tyrant, whose successes
Makes heaven unfear'd, and villainy assured
Beyond its power there's nothing; almost puts
Faith in a fever, and deifies alone
Voluble chance; who only attributes
The faculties of other instruments
To his own nerves and act; commands men service,
And what they win in't, boot and glory; one
That fears not to do harm; good, dares not. Let
The blood of mine that's sib to him be suck'd
From me with leeches! Let them break and fall
Off me with that corruption!

ARCITE
Clear-spirited cousin,
Let's leave his court, that we may nothing share
Of his loud infamy; for our milk
Will relish of the pasture, and we must
Be vile, or disobedient—not his kinsmen
In blood unless in quality.

PALAMON
Nothing truer.
I think the echoes of his shames have deaf'd
The ears of heav'nly justice. Widows' cries
Descend again into their throats, and have not
Due audience of the gods.

Valerius!

VALERIUS
The King calls for you; yet be leaden-footed
Till his great rage be off him. Phoebus, when
He broke his whipstock and exclaim'd against
The horses of the sun, but whisper'd, to

don't need treatment; the one which almost tears my heart out is–

Our uncle Creon.

*Him,
the most unrestrained tyrant, his successes have made him fearless and ensured his villainy thinks that there is nothing beyond his power; he almost destroys faith, and claims that he can beat chance; something that has been done by others he takes the credit for, insisting it was his own nerves and actions which succeeded; he orders men to fight and takes the rewards and the glory; he never hesitates to do harm and dares not do good. Let that part of my blood which is related to him be sucked out of me with leeches! Let them die and fall off me, taking that pollution!*

*Pure souled cousin,
let's leave his court, so we don't become associated with his terrible reputation; what we do will be influenced by where we are, and we shall have to be vile, or disobedient–we won't be seen as one of the family unless we are the same as him.*

*You're quite right.
I think the sound of his shameful deeds have deafened the ears of the judges of heaven. The cries of widows sink back into their throats, and are not being properly listened to by the gods.*

Enter Valerius.

Valerius!

The King is calling for you; but go there slowly, wait for his anger to die down. When Phoebus broke his whip and shouted out against the horses of the sun, he was just whispering,

22

The loudness of his fury.

compared to the loudness of the King's rage.

PALAMON
Small winds shake him.
But what's the matter?

The smallest thing upsets him.
But what is it this time?

VALERIUS
Theseus (who where he threats appalls) hath sent
Deadly defiance to him, and pronounces
Ruin to Thebes; who is at hand to seal
The promise of his wrath.

Theseus (who is whom he is cursing) has sent
him a deadly challenge, and announced that he
is going to destroy Thebes; he is close by,
intending to keep this promise.

ARCITE
Let him approach.
But that we fear the gods in him, he brings not
A jot of terror to us. Yet what man
Thirds his own worth (the case is each of ours),
When that his action's dregg'd with mind assur'd
'Tis bad he goes about.

Let him come on.
Apart from the gods he represents, we are not
at all afraid of him. But how a man
reduces his own worth (this is the case with us)
when he does something with his mind clouded
by the
thought that what he's doing is bad.

PALAMON
Leave that unreason'd.
Our services stand now for Thebes, not Creon.
Yet to be neutral to him were dishonor;
Rebellious to oppose; therefore we must
With him stand to the mercy of our fate,
Who hath bounded our last minute.

Don't think of it that way.
We are going to fight for Thebes, not Creon.
It would be dishonourable to claim neutrality;
it would be rebellious to oppose him; and so we
must put our luck to the test with him,
who has command of us.

ARCITE
So we must.
Is't said this war's afoot? Or it shall be,
On fail of some condition?

Yes we must.
Has the war actually begun? Or will it be
when some condition isn't met?

VALERIUS
'Tis in motion,
The intelligence of state came in the instant
With the defier.

It's begun,
the information from the spies came in at the
same moment as the declaration from Theseus.

PALAMON
Let's to the King, who were he
A quarter carrier of that honor which
His enemy come in, the blood we venture
Should be as for our health, which were not spent,

Let's go to the King, if he was
a quarter as honourable as
his enemy, the blood we are risking
would actually be good for us,
it would not be lost,

23

Rather laid out for purchase. But alas,
Our hands advanc'd before our hearts, what will
The fall o' th' stroke do damage?

ARCITE
Let th' event,
That never-erring arbitrator, tell us
When we know all ourselves, and let us follow
The becking of our chance.

we would actually gain from it. But alas,
with our hands acting against our instincts,
how will we suffer for our wounds?

Let's allow time,
that never failing umpire, to show us
when we have seen how everything turns out,
and let's just take our chances.

Scene III

Before the gates of Athens.

(Pirithous, Hippolyta, Emilia)

Enter Pirithous, Hippolyta, Emilia.

PIRITHOUS
No further.

HIPPOLYTA
Sir, farewell. Repeat my wishes
To our great lord, of whose success I dare not
Make any timorous question; yet I wish him
Excess and overflow of power, and't might be,
To dure ill-dealing fortune. Speed to him,
Store never hurts good governors.

PIRITHOUS
Though I know
His ocean needs not my poor drops, yet they
Must yield their tribute there. My precious
maid,
Those best affections that the heavens infuse
In their best-temper'd pieces, keep enthron'd
In your dear heart!

EMILIA
Thanks, sir. Remember me
To our all-royal brother, for whose speed
The great Bellona I'll solicit; and
Since in our terrene state petitions are not
Without gifts understood, I'll offer to her
What I shall be advis'd she likes. Our hearts
Are in his army, in his tent.

HIPPOLYTA
In 's bosom.
We have been soldiers, and we cannot weep
When our friends don their helms, or put to sea,
Or tell of babes broach'd on the lance, or
women
That have sod their infants in (and after eat

This is as far as I go.

Sir, farewell. Carry my good wishes
to our great lord, whose success I dare not
call into question; but I wish him
all the power he needs and more, so if
necessary he can overcome any bad luck. Take
this to him quickly, abundance never harmed
careful men.

Although I know
his ocean of goodness does not need my tiny
drops, I must still give them to him. My dear
girl, keep all that love, which is touched with
all the best things of heaven, worshipped
in your dear heart!

Thank you, sir. Give my greetings
to our most royal brother, for whose success I
will pray to the goddess of war; and as
our earthly petitions are not heard without
gifts, I'll sacrifice to her whatever I'm told she
likes. Our hearts are with his army, in his tent.

Within his heart.
We have been soldiers, and we cannot weep
when our friends put on their helmets, or set
sail, or tell us of babies spitted on lances, all
women who have preserved their children in
the salt tears

them)
The brine they wept at killing 'em. Then if
You stay to see of us such spinsters, we
Should hold you here forever.

PIRITHOUS
Peace be to you
As I pursue this war, which shall be then
Beyond further requiring.

EMILIA
How his longing
Follows his friend: since his depart, his sports,
Though craving seriousness and skill, pass'd
slightly
His careless execution, where nor gain
Made him regard, or loss consider, but
Playing o'er business in his hand, another
Directing in his head, his mind nurse equal
To these so diff'ring twins. Have you observ'd
him
Since our great lord departed?

HIPPOLYTA
With much labor;
And I did love him for't. They two have
cabin'd
In many as dangerous as poor a corner,
Peril and want contending, they have skiff'd
Torrents whose roaring tyranny and power
I' th' least of these was dreadful, and they have
Fought out together where death's self was
lodg'd;
Yet fate hath brought them off. Their knot of
love
Tied, weav'd, entangled, with so true, so long,
And with a finger of so deep a cunning,
May be outworn, never undone. I think
Theseus cannot be umpire to himself,
Cleaving his conscience into twain and doing
Each side like justice, which he loves best.

EMILIA
Doubtless
There is a best, and reason has no manners

*they wept when they killed them (and then ate
them). If you waited here to see us being such
timid women, you would wait here forever.*

*May peace be with you
while I go to war, I shall not
be needing it there.*

Exit Pirithous.

*How his desires
follow his friend; since he left, his amusements,
though they were frivolous and without skill,
seemed to mean nothing to him, he didn't
care about winning or losing, he had
one matter in front of him in his hand and
another
turning over in his mind, he had two things
there at once. Have you noticed him
since our great lord left?*

*He was much upset;
and I loved him for it. Those two have been
together in many a tight spot,
dangerous and deprived, they have rowed over
rapids where tyranny and power
roared dreadfully, and they have
fought together in the shadow of death;
but fate let them live. The knot of their love
is so deeply intertwined, tied with such
skill and cunning that it will outlive them,
it can never be undone. I think
Theseus could not decide between them,
it would be like splitting himself in half and
trying to decide which side he loved best.*

*No doubt
there is a side he loves best,*

To say it is not you. I was acquainted
Once with a time when I enjoy'd a playfellow;
You were at wars when she the grave enrich'd,
Who made too proud the bed, took leave o' th'
moon
(Which then look'd pale at parting) when our
count
Was each aleven.

HIPPOLYTA
'Twas Flavina.

EMILIA
Yes.
You talk of Pirithous' and Theseus' love:
Theirs has more ground, is more maturely
season'd,
More buckled with strong judgment, and their
needs
The one of th' other may be said to water
Their intertangled roots of love, but I
And she (I sigh and spoke of) were things
innocent,
Lov'd for we did, and like the elements
That know not what nor why, yet do effect
Rare issues by their operance, our souls
Did so to one another. What she lik'd
Was then of me approv'd, what not,
condemn'd,
No more arraignment. The flow'r that I would
pluck
And put between my breasts (O then but
beginning
To swell about the blossom), she would long
Till she had such another, and commit it
To the like innocent cradle, where phoenix-like
They died in perfume. On my head no toy
But was her pattern, her affections (pretty,
Though happily her careless wear) I followed
For my most serious decking. Had mine ear
Stol'n some new air, or at adventure humm'd
one
From musical coinage, why, it was a note
Whereon her spirits would sojourn (rather
dwell on)
And sing it in her slumbers. This rehearsal

and one would certainly say that side is you.
There was a time once
when I had a playmate;
you were at the wars when she went to her
grave, which was all too ready to receive her,
said goodbye to the moon
(which looked pale at her going) when we were
each eleven years old.

You're talking of Flavina.

Yes.
You talk of the love of Pirithous and Theseus:
theirs has a more solid basis, has grown
through time,
has been strengthened through adult
judgement, and the
needs they have of each other could be said to
water
the entwined roots of their love, but she
and I (I sigh to speak of her) were innocents,
simply loved without reason, like the stars
that have no knowledge of how or why but still
affect great issues in their motions, that was
what
our souls were like to one another. What she
liked
I immediately liked, what she didn't, I hated
without question. If I plucked a flower
and put it between my breasts (which were then
just
beginning to grow) she would pine
until she had one just the same, and put it
into the same innocent holder, where they
would die
releasing their perfume. I wouldn't wear a hat
that wasn't like hers, her fashions (pretty,
even when she had just thrown something on) I
followed
for my most formal wear. If I heard
some new tune, or perhaps hummed one
of my own invention, why, she would
take it into her heart
and sing it in her sleep. This story

(Which, ev'ry innocent wots well, comes in
Like old importment's bastard) has this end,
That the true love 'tween maid and maid may be
More than in sex dividual.

HIPPOLYTA
Y' are out of breath,
And this high-speeded pace is but to say
That you shall never (like the maid Flavina)
Love any that's call'd man.

EMILIA
I am sure I shall not.

HIPPOLYTA
Now alack, weak sister,
I must no more believe thee in this point
(Though in't I know thou dost believe thyself)
Than I will trust a sickly appetite,
That loathes even as it longs. But sure, my sister,
If I were ripe for your persuasion, you
Have said enough to shake me from the arm
Of the all-noble Theseus, for whose fortunes
I will now in and kneel, with great assurance
That we, more than his Pirithous, possess
The high throne in his heart.

EMILIA
I am not
Against your faith, yet I continue mine.

*(which every simpleton can see produces
great emotion in me) has this moral,
that true love between two girls may be
greater than between men and women.*

*You are out of breath,
and your rushing words tell me
that you will never love a man
as you loved the girl Flavina.*

I am sure I shall not.

*Now alas, weak sister,
I don't give any more credence to you on this
(although I know that you believe it is true)
then I would give to the appetite of an invalid,
that craves things even though they would
sicken it. I can assure you, my sister, if I could
be persuaded, you have said enough to pull me
away from the great noble Theseus, for whom I
will now go in and pray, safe in the knowledge
that I, not his Pirithous, hold the
highest place in his heart.*

*I won't
argue with you, though I still believe what I
said.*

Exeunt.

Scene IV

A field before Thebes.

(Theseus, Lords, Three Queens, Herald, Attendants, Palamon, Arcite)

Cornets. A battle strook within; then a retreat; flourish.
Then enter Theseus, victor, with his Lords. The three Queens meet him and fall on their faces
before him.

FIRST QUEEN
To thee no star be dark.

May the stars always shine on you.

SECOND QUEEN
Both heaven and earth
Friend thee forever.

May Heaven and Earth
always be your friends.

THIRD QUEEN
All the good that may
Be wish'd upon thy head, I cry amen to't.

I pray for all good things
to fall upon your head.

THESEUS
Th' impartial gods, who from the mounted heavens
View us their mortal herd, behold who err,
And in their time chastise. Go and find out
The bones of your dead lords, and honor them
With treble ceremony; rather than a gap
Should be in their dear rites, we would supply't.
But those we will depute which shall invest
You in your dignities, and even each thing
Our haste does leave imperfect. So adieu,
And heaven's good eyes look on you!

The impartial gods, who look down from
heaven to see us, their mortal flock, see who
does wrong, and in the fullness of time punish
them. Go find the bodies of your dead lords,
and perform the funeral rites three times over;
rather than anything being missing in the
ceremony, I would gladly perform them myself.
But those I shall order to do it will
make sure it's done with dignity, and they will
make sure that anything I have left undone in
my hurry is corrected. So goodbye,
and may the gods look upon you favourably!

What are those?

Who are those people?

Exeunt Queens.

Enter Herald with Attendants bearing Palamon and Arcite on two hearses.
Men of great quality, as may be judg'd
By their appointment. Some of Thebes have

HERALD

They are men of great quality, you can tell
by their clothes. Some of the Thebans told me

told's
They are sisters' children, nephews to the King.

THESEUS
By th' helm of Mars, I saw them in the war,
Like to a pair of lions smear'd with prey,
Make lanes in troops aghast. I fix'd my note
Constantly on them; for they were a mark
Worth a god's view. What was't that prisoner
told me
When I inquired their names?

HERALD
Wi' leave, they're called
Arcite and Palamon.

THESEUS
'Tis right—those, those.
They are not dead?

HERALD
Nor in a state of life; had they been taken
When their last hurts were given, 'twas possible
They might have been recovered. Yet they
breathe
And have the name of men.

THESEUS
Then like men use 'em.
The very lees of such (millions of rates)
Exceed the wine of others. All our surgeons
Convent in their behoof, our richest balms,
Rather than niggard, waste; their lives concern
us
Much more than Thebes is worth. Rather than
have 'em
Freed of this plight, and in their morning state
(Sound and at liberty), I would 'em dead;
But forty thousand fold we had rather have 'em
Prisoners to us than death. Bear 'em speedily
From our kind air, to them unkind, and minister
What man to man may do; for our sake more,
Since I have known frights, fury, friends'
behests,
Love's provocations, zeal, a mistress' task,
Desire of liberty, a fever, madness,

*that they are children of his sister, nephews to
the King.*

*By the helmet of Mars, I saw them in the war,
they were like a pair of lions attacking their
prey, cutting paths through the terrified troops.
I watched them constantly, for they were
worthy of being watched by gods. What did that
prisoner say to me
when I asked their names?*

*If you please, they are called
Arcite and Palamon.*

*That's right, those are the ones.
They're not dead?*

*They are hardly alive; had they been captured
at the time they got their last wounds, it might
have been possible for them to recover. But
they are still breathing
and can still be called men.*

*Then treat them like men.
The very dregs of such men are a million times
better than the wine of others. Gather all of
our doctors to work on them, it would be better
to waste our best medicines than be sparing
with them; their lives are more important to me
than all of Thebes. Rather than them being
out of danger and in the same position they
were in this morning
(healthy and free), I would rather they were
dead; but I would forty thousand times prefer to
have them as my prisoners rather than dead.
Take them away quickly from this place which
hasn't been good to them, and do everything for
them a man can for another; for my sake do
more, since I have known fear, fury, the
requests of friends, the pains of love, anger, the
scolding of a mistress, the desire for freedom, a*

Hath set a mark which nature could not reach to
Without some imposition, sickness in will
O'er-wrastling strength in reason. For our love,
And great Apollo's mercy, all our best
Their best skill tender.—Lead into the city,
Where having bound things scatter'd, we will
post
To Athens 'fore our army.

*fever, madness, which could not be suffered
without leaving some scars, the sickness of
desire overcoming the strength of reason. Out
of love for me, and to gain mercy from great
Apollo, tell all our best men to do their best.
Lead us into the city, and when we have
gathered together our forces, I will ride
to Athens at the head of my army.*

Flourish. Exeunt, Attendants bearing Palamon and Arcite.

Scene V

Another part of a field before Thebes.

(Three Queens, Knights)

Music. Enter the Queens with the hearses of their Knights in a funeral solemnity, etc.

Urns and odors bring away,
Vapors, sighs, darken the day;
Our dole more deadly looks than dying;
Balms, and gums, and heavy cheers,
Sacred vials fill'd with tears,
And clamors through the wild air flying!
Come all sad and solemn shows,
That are quick-ey'd pleasure's foes!
We convent nought else but woes:
We convent, etc.

Song.
Carry away the urns and incense,
Tears and sighs darken the day;
our grief looks more deadly than death itself;
with medicines, and potions and great cries,
holy vials filled with tears,
with cries ringing through the stormy air!
Come all demonstrations of sadness,
the opposites to bright eyed pleasure!
Nothing but sorrow is gathering here.

THIRD QUEEN
This funeral path brings to your household's grave:
Joy seize on you again! Peace sleep with him!

This funeral route brings you to your family grave:
May you be happy again! Rest in peace!

SECOND QUEEN
And this to yours.

And the same to yours.

FIRST QUEEN
Yours this way. Heavens lend
A thousand differing ways to one sure end.

And to yours. The heavens give us
a thousand different ways to come to one certain end.

THIRD QUEEN
This world's a city full of straying streets,
And death's the market-place, where each one meets.

This world is a city full of wandering streets,
and death is the marketplace, where they all meet.

Exeunt severally.

Act II

Scene I

Athens. A garden, with a prison in the background.

(Jailer, Wooer, Daughter, Palamon, Arcite)

Enter Jailer and Wooer.

JAILER
I may depart with little, while I live; something I may cast to you, not much. Alas, the prison I keep, though it be for great ones, yet they seldom come: before one salmon, you shall take a number of minnows. I am given out to be better lin'd than it can appear to me report is a true speaker. I would I were really that I am deliver'd to be. Marry, what I have (be it what it will) I will assure upon my daughter at the day of my death.

I can't give much away, while I'm alive; I might be able to give you something, not much. Alas, although the prison I run is for noblemen, I don't often get them: you catch many more minnows than salmon. The rumours say I am much wealthier than I actually am. I wish I had what they say I have. Still, whatever I have, whatever it is, I promise to my daughter on the day I die.

WOOER
Sir, I demand no more than your own offer, and I will estate your daughter in what I have promis'd.

Sir, I want nothing more than what you have offered, and I will settle what I have promised on your daughter.

JAILER
Well, we will talk more of this when the solemnity is past. But have you a full promise of her? When that shall be seen, I tender my consent.

Well, we will talk more of this when the serious business is over. But have you got her full agreement? When I see that, I'll give my consent.

Enter Daughter with strewings.

WOOER
I have, sir. Here she comes.

I have, sir. Here she comes.

JAILER
Your friend and I have chanc'd to name you here, upon the old business. But no more of that now; so soon as the court hurry is over, we will have an end of it. I' th' mean time, look tenderly to the
two prisoners. I can tell you they are princes.

Your friend and I happened to be talking about you, on the usual matter. But enough of that for now; as soon as all this commotion at court is over we will settle the matter. In the meantime, look after the two prisoners carefully. I can tell you they are princes.

JAILER'S DAUGHTER

These strewings are for their chamber. 'Tis pity they are in prison, and 'twere pity they should be out. I do think they have patience to make any adversity asham'd. The prison itself is proud of 'em; and they have all the world in their chamber.

JAILER
They are fam'd to be a pair of absolute men.

JAILER'S DAUGHTER
By my troth, I think fame but stammers 'em, they stand a grise above the reach of report.

JAILER
I heard them reported in the battle to be the only doers.

JAILER'S DAUGHTER
Nay, most likely, for they are noble suff'rers. I marvel how they would have look'd had they been victors, that with such a constant nobility enforce a freedom out of bondage, making misery their mirth, and affliction a toy to jest at.

JAILER
Do they so?

JAILER'S DAUGHTER
It seems to me they have no more sense of their captivity than I of ruling Athens. They eat well, look merrily, discourse of many things, but nothing of their own restraint and disasters. Yet sometime a divided sigh, martyr'd as 'twere i' th' deliverance, will break from one of them; when the other presently gives it so sweet a rebuke that I could wish myself a sigh to be so chid, or at least a sigher to be comforted.

WOOER
I never saw 'em.

JAILER
The Duke himself came privately in the night, and so did they. What the reason of it is, I know not.

These flowers are for their room. It's a shame they are in prison, and it would be a shame if they weren't. I think may have the patience to suffer any adversity. The prison is proud to have them as guests, and everybody visits their room.

They are said to be a pair of wonderful men.

I swear their reputation isn't good enough, they are head and shoulders above what they are said to be.

I heard it said that they were the only ones fighting in the battle.

That's very likely, for they are very noble in their suffering. I'm amazed to think what they would have been like if they had won, when they so nobly seem to be free in their imprisonment, laughing in their misery, and joking at their wounds.

Is that what they do?

They seem to have no more idea that they are captives than I would have of ruling Athens. They eat well, look happy, talk of many things, but they don't say anything about their own imprisonment and misfortunes. But sometimes one of them will give a stifled sigh, choked off even as it breaks out; then the other will rebuke it so sweetly that it makes me wish I was a sigh to be criticised like that, or at least a sigher to receive such comfort.

I never saw them.

The Duke himself came privately at night, and so did they. What the reason is for that, I don't know.

Enter Palamon and Arcite above.

Look yonder they are! That's Arcite looks out.

JAILER'S DAUGHTER
No, sir, no, that's Palamon. Arcite is the lower of the twain; you may perceive a part of him.

JAILER
Go to, leave your pointing. They would not make us their object. Out of their sight.

JAILER'S DAUGHTER
It is a holiday to look on them. Lord, the diff'rence of men!

Enter Palamon and Arcite above.

Look, they are up there! That's Arcite looking out.

No, sir, no, that's Palamon. Arcite is the shorter of the two; you can see part of him.

Come on, stop pointing at them. They don't want us staring at them. Lets get out of their sight.

It's like a holiday to look at them. Lord, how different men can be!

Exeunt Jailer, Wooer, and Daughter.

Shall we two exercise, like twins of honor,
Our arms again, and feel our fiery horses

Scene II

The prison.

(Palamon, Arcite, Emilia, Woman, Jailer)

Enter Palamon, and Arcite in prison.

PALAMON
How do you, noble cousin?

ARCITE
How do you, sir?

PALAMON
Why, strong enough to laugh at misery
And bear the chance of war yet. We are
prisoners
I fear forever, cousin.

ARCITE
I believe it,
And to that destiny have patiently
Laid up my hour to come.

PALAMON
O cousin Arcite,
Where is Thebes now? Where is our noble
country?
Where are our friends and kindreds? Never
more
Must we behold those comforts, never see
The hardy youths strive for the games of honor,
Hung with the painted favors of their ladies,
Like tall ships under sail; then start amongst
'em
And as an east wind leave 'em all behind us,
Like lazy clouds, whilst Palamon and Arcite,
Even in the wagging of a wanton leg,
Outstripp'd the people's praises, won the
garlands,
Ere they have time to wish 'em ours. O, never

Like proud seas under us. Our good swords now
(Better the red-ey'd god of war nev'r ware),
Ravish'd our sides, like age must run to rust,
And deck the temples of those gods that hate us;
These hands shall never draw 'em out like lightning
To blast whole armies more.

ARCITE
No, Palamon,
Those hopes are prisoners with us. Here we are,
And here the graces of our youths must wither
Like a too-timely spring. Here age must find us,
And which is heaviest, Palamon, unmarried.
The sweet embraces of a loving wife,
Loaden with kisses, arm'd with thousand Cupids,
Shall never clasp our necks; no issue know us;
No figures of ourselves shall we ev'r see
To glad our age, and like young eagles teach 'em
Boldly to gaze against bright arms, and say,
"Remember what your fathers were, and conquer!"
The fair-ey'd maids shall weep our banishments,
And in their songs curse ever-blinded Fortune
Till she for shame see what a wrong she has done
To youth and nature. This is all our world:
We shall know nothing here but one another,
Hear nothing but the clock that tells our woes;
The vine shall grow, but we shall never see it;
Summer shall come, and with her all delights,
But dead-cold winter must inhabit here still.

PALAMON
'Tis too true, Arcite. To our Theban hounds,
That shook the aged forest with their echoes,
No more now must we hallow; no more shake
Our pointed javelins, whilst the angry swine
Flies like a Parthian quiver from our rages,
Struck with our well-steel'd darts. All valiant uses

How are you, noble cousin?

How are you, sir?

Well, strong enough to laugh at misery and endure the fortunes of war. I fear that we are to stay in prison forever, cousin.

I believe it, and I have set myself to patiently endure that fate.

Oh cousin Arcite, where is Thebes now? Where is our noble country? Where our friends and family? Will we never see those sweet things again, never see the robust youths jousting, carrying the painted banners of their ladies, like tall ships with their sails hoisted; then we would charge amongst them and leave them all behind us like an east wind leaves the lazy clouds, whilst Palamon and Arcite, in the twinkling of an eye, surpassed the praises people gave them, won the prizes, before they even had time to say they should be ours. Oh, we two shall never get to show off our weapons again, embodiments of honour, or feel our fiery horses heaving like great seas underneath us. Now our good swords (Mars himself never carried a better one),

torn from our sides, must turn to rust like old
men,
and decorate the temples of the gods who hate
us;
these hands will never flash them out like
lightning
to cut down great armies.

No, Palamon,
those hopes are imprisoned with us. Here we
are, and here the beauty of our youth must fade
like a too early spring. Here we will grow old,
and what is worse, Palamon, we will do so
unmarried. The sweet embraces of a loving
wife, loaded with kisses, backed up by a
thousand cupids, will never be thrown round
our necks; no children will know us;
we shall see no copies of ourselves
to brighten up our old age, and to teach them
like young eagles to boldly face the glare of the
enemy's weapons, and say, "Remember who
your fathers were, and win!" The beautiful girls
will cry over our exile, and in their songs they
will curse eternally blind fortune, until she is
shamed into seeing what a wrong she has done
against youth and nature. This is our whole
world:
we shall know nobody here but each other,
hear nothing but the clock ticking out our
sorrows;
the vines will grow, but we shall never see
them;
summer will come, with all her delights,
but it will always be the dead of winter in here.

That's too true, Arcite. We can no longer call
to our Theban hounds, who shook the ancient
forests with their barking; no more will we
shake our sharp javelins, while the angry boar
runs like a Parthian from our attacks,
carrying our trusty arrows. All brave qualities
(the food and nourishment of noble minds)

(The food and nourishment of noble minds)
In us two here shall perish; we shall die
(Which is the curse of honor) lastly
Children of grief and ignorance.

ARCITE
Yet, cousin,
Even from the bottom of these miseries,
From all that fortune can inflict upon us,
I see two comforts rising, two mere blessings,
If the gods please—to hold here a brave
patience,
And the enjoying of our griefs together.
Whilst Palamon is with me, let me perish
If I think this our prison.

PALAMON
Certainly
'Tis a main goodness, cousin, that our fortunes
Were twin'd together. 'Tis most true, two souls
Put in two noble bodies, let 'em suffer
The gall of hazard, so they grow together,
Will never sink; they must not, say they could;
A willing man dies sleeping, and all's done.

ARCITE
Shall we make worthy uses of this place
That all men hate so much?

PALAMON
How, gentle cousin?

ARCITE
Let's think this prison holy sanctuary
To keep us from corruption of worse men.
We are young and yet desire the ways of honor,
That liberty and common conversation,
The poison of pure spirits, might, like women,
Woo us to wander from. What worthy blessing
Can be, but our imaginations
May make it ours? And here being thus
together,
We are an endless mine to one another;
We are one another's wife, ever begetting
New births of love; we are father, friends,
acquaintance;

will die here in us; we shall die
(this is the curse of honour) finally,
full of grief and ignorance.

But, cousin,
even in the depths of these miseries,
suffering all the worst that fortune can throw at
us, I can see two comforts, two perfect
blessings, if the gods allow them–that we can
use to reconcile ourselves
to our fate and face our sorrows together.
Whilst Palamon is with me, let me die
if I think of this as our prison.

It's certainly
a great stroke of luck, cousin, that our fates
were joined together. It's very true, two souls
in two noble bodies, let them suffer
the spite of fate, as long as they are together,
they will never sink; they must not, even if they
could; when a man wants to he dies in his
sleep, and that's the end.

Shall we make good use of this place
that all men hate so much?

How, gentle cousin?

Let's think of this prison as a holy sanctuary,
to keep us from being corrupted by bad men.
We are young and yet we want to follow the
paths of honour, which freedom and low talk,
the curse of pure natures, might, like women,
lead us astray from. What is there that can't
become a blessing, if we just imagine
that it is? And as we are here together,
we are never-ending resources to each other;
we are each the wife of the other, forever
creating new children of love; we are father,
friends, acquaintances; we are each other's
families:

We are, in one another, families:
I am your heir, and you are mine; this place
Is our inheritance. No hard oppressor
Dare take this from us; here with a little patience
We shall live long, and loving. No surfeits seek us;
The hand of war hurts none here, nor the seas
Swallow their youth. Were we at liberty,
A wife might part us lawfully, or business,
Quarrels consume us, envy of ill men
Crave our acquaintance; I might sicken, cousin,
Where you should never know it, and so perish
Without your noble hand to close mine eyes,
Or prayers to the gods. A thousand chances,
Were we from hence, would sever us.

PALAMON
You have made me
(I thank you, cousin Arcite) almost wanton
With my captivity. What a misery
It is to live abroad, and every where!
'Tis like a beast, methinks. I find the court here,
I am sure, a more content, and all those pleasures
That woo the wills of men to vanity
I see through now, and am sufficient
To tell the world 'tis but a gaudy shadow
That old Time, as he passes by, takes with him.
What had we been, old in the court of Creon,
Where sin is justice, lust and ignorance
The virtues of the great ones? Cousin Arcite,
Had not the loving gods found this place for us,
We had died as they do, ill old men, unwept,
And had their epitaphs, the people's curses.
Shall I say more?

ARCITE
I would hear you still.

PALAMON
Ye shall.
Is there record of any two that lov'd
Better than we do, Arcite?
ARCITE
Sure there cannot.

I am your heir, and you are mine; this place is our inheritance. No hard oppressor would dare to take this away from us; with a little patience we shall live long and loving lives here. There will be no excess; nobody can be hurt by war here, nor can they be drowned in the sea. If we were free, a wife might lawfully separate us, or we might quarrel over money, fall in with bad companions; I might become ill, cousin, and you would never know it, and so I would die without your noble hand to close my eyes, or offer prayers to the gods. If we weren't here, a thousand different things could separate us.

You have made me (I thank you, cousin Arcite) almost love my imprisonment. How miserable it is to live in the wide world, go everywhere! That's like being an animal, I think. I'm sure that our position here is a more contented one, and I can see through all those pleasures which attract men to frivolous things, and I'm able to tell the world that these things are just vulgar shadows that disappear with the passing of time. What would we have become, grown old in Creon's court, where sin rules and lust and ignorance are the virtues of great men? Cousin Arcite, if the loving gods hadn't found this place for us, we would have died like them, sick old men, unmourned, with the curses of the people as our epitaphs. Shall I say more?

Do go on.

*I shall.
Have you ever heard of any two who loved each other better than us, Arcite?*

I'm sure there can't have been.

PALAMON
I do not think it possible our friendship
Should ever leave us.

I don't think it's possible for our friendship to ever end.

ARCITE
Till our deaths it cannot,

It cannot until we die,

Enter Emilia and her Woman below.

And after death our spirits shall be led
To those that love eternally. Speak on, sir.

and after death our spirits will
It cannot until we die, and after death our spirits will

EMILIA
This garden has a world of pleasures in't.
What flow'r is this?

This garden is full of pleasures.
What's this flower?

WAITING-WOMAN
'Tis call'd narcissus, madam.

That's called Narcissus, madam.

EMILIA
That was a fair boy certain, but a fool
To love himself. Were there not maids enough?

He was certainly good-looking boy, but a fool to love himself. Weren't there enough girls for him?

ARCITE
Pray forward.

Please go on.

PALAMON
Yes.

Yes.

EMILIA
Or were they all hard-hearted?

Or were they all hardhearted?

WAITING-WOMAN
They could not be to one so fair.

They couldn't have hardened their hearts against one so beautiful.

EMILIA
Thou wouldst not.

You wouldn't have.

WAITING-WOMAN
I think I should not, madam.

Definitely not, madam.

EMILIA
That's a good wench!
But take heed to your kindness though.

Good lass!
But watch yourself with your kindness.

WAITING-WOMAN

44

Why, madam?

EMILIA
Men are mad things.

ARCITE
Will ye go forward, cousin?

EMILIA
Canst not thou work such flowers in silk, wench?

WAITING-WOMAN
Yes.

EMILIA
I'll have a gown full of 'em, and of these:
This is a pretty color, will't not do
Rarely upon a skirt, wench?

WAITING-WOMAN
Dainty, madam.

ARCITE
Cousin, cousin, how do you, sir? Why,
Palamon!

PALAMON
Never till now I was in prison, Arcite.

ARCITE
Why, what's the matter, man?

PALAMON
Behold, and wonder!
By heaven, she is a goddess.

ARCITE
Ha!

PALAMON
Do reverence;
She is a goddess, Arcite.

EMILIA
Of all flow'rs

Why, madam?

Because men are mad.

Will you carry on, cousin?

Can you embroider these flowers on silk, girl?

Yes.

I'll have a dress covered in them, and these: this is a pretty colour; don't you think it would look very good on a skirt, girl?

Very sweet, madam.

Cousin, cousin, how are you, sir? Why, Palamon!

I never felt I was in prison until now, Arcite.

Why, what's the matter, man?

*Look, and be amazed!
By heaven, she is a goddess.*

Ha!

*Worship her;
she is a goddess, Arcite.*

I think that roses

45

Methinks a rose is best.

WAITING-WOMAN
Why, gentle madam?

EMILIA
It is the very emblem of a maid;
For when the west wind courts her gently,
How modestly she blows, and paints the sun
With her chaste blushes! When the north comes
near her,
Rude and impatient, then, like chastity,
She locks her beauties in her bud again,
And leaves him to base briers.

WAITING-WOMAN
Yet, good madam,
Sometimes her modesty will blow so far she
falls for't.
A maid, if she have any honor, would be loath
To take example by her.

EMILIA
Thou art wanton.

ARCITE
She is wondrous fair.

PALAMON
She is all the beauty extant.

EMILIA
The sun grows high, let's walk in. Keep these
flowers,
We'll see how near art can come near their
colors.
I am wondrous merry-hearted, I could laugh
now.

WAITING-WOMAN
I could lie down, I am sure.

EMILIA
And take one with you?

WAITING-WOMAN

are the best of all the flowers.

Why, sweet madam?

She perfectly symbolises a maid;
for when the West wind gently approaches her,
how modestly she opens up, adorning the sun
with her chaste blushes! When the north wind
comes near her,
rude and bullying, then, like chastity,
she locks her beauties up in her bud again,
and leaves him with the low thorns.

Yet, good madam,
sometimes in her modesty she will blow over so
far she actually falls.
Any girl who has any honour would not wish
to follow her example.

You are lusty.

She's incredibly beautiful.

She is everything beautiful in the world.

The sun's getting high, let's go indoors. Keep
these flowers,
we'll see how closely art can match their
colours.
I feel very happy, I could laugh now.

I think I could lie down.

Taking someone with you?

That's as we bargain, madam.

That can be negotiated, madam.

EMILIA
Well, agree then.

Well, agree to it then.

Exeunt Emilia and Woman.

PALAMON
What think you of this beauty?

What do you think of this beauty?

ARCITE
'Tis a rare one.

She is exceptional.

PALAMON
Is't but a rare one?

Just exceptional?

ARCITE
Yes, a matchless beauty.

Yes, an incomparable beauty.

PALAMON
Might not a man well lose himself and love
her?

*Couldn't a man easily lose himself and fall in
love with her?*

ARCITE
I cannot tell what you have done; I have,
Beshrew mine eyes for't! Now I feel my
shackles.

*I can't tell what you have done; I have,
damn my eyes for doing it! Now I can feel my
chains.*

PALAMON
You love her then?

You love her then?

ARCITE
Who would not?

Who wouldn't?

PALAMON
And desire her?

And you desire her?

ARCITE
Before my liberty.

More than my freedom.

PALAMON
I saw her first.

I saw her first.

ARCITE
That's nothing.

That doesn't count for anything.

PALAMON

But it shall be.

It will do.

ARCITE
I saw her too.

I saw her as well.

PALAMON
Yes, but you must not love her.

Yes, but you must not love her.

ARCITE
I will not, as you do—to worship her
As she is heavenly and a blessed goddess;
I love her as a woman, to enjoy her.
So both may love.

*I won't, not in the same way you do,
worshipping her as a heavenly and blessed
goddess; I love her as a woman, I want to enjoy
her. So we can both love.*

PALAMON
You shall not love at all.

You shan't love at all.

ARCITE
Not love at all! Who shall deny me?

Not love at all! Who's going to stop me?

PALAMON
I, that first saw her; I, that took possession
First with mine eye of all those beauties in her
Reveal'd to mankind. If thou lov'st her,
Or entertain'st a hope to blast my wishes,
Thou art a traitor, Arcite, and a fellow
False as thy title to her. Friendship, blood,
And all the ties between us, I disclaim
If thou once think upon her.

*Me, who saw her first; me, who first
took possession with my eyes of all that beauty
that mankind can see. If you love her,
or hope to defeat my ambitions,
you are a traitor, Arcite, and a man
as illegitimate as your claim on her. If you
so much as think about her just once, I disown
our friendship, our kinship and all the ties
between us.*

ARCITE
Yes, I love her,
And if the lives of all my name lay on it,
I must do so; I love her with my soul;
If that will lose ye, farewell, Palamon.
I say again, I love, and in loving her maintain
I am as worthy and as free a lover,
And have as just a title to her beauty,
As any Palamon or any living
That is a man's son.

*Yes, I love her,
and I would have to do so if the lives
of my entire family depended on it;
I love her with my soul; if that means we part
then farewell, Palamon. I tell you again, I love
her, and in loving her I insist that I am just as
worthy and just as free to love her, and have an
equal claim to her beauty, as any Palamon or
any living human being.*

PALAMON
Have I call'd thee friend?

Did I call you my friend?

ARCITE
Yes, and have found me so. Why are you

Yes, and I have been. Why are you so upset?

mov'd thus?
Let me deal coldly with you: am not I
Part of your blood, part of your soul? You have told me
That I was Palamon, and you were Arcite.

*Let me speak plainly to you: I'm not
part of your blood, part of your soul? You have told me
that I was Palamon, and you were Arcite.*

PALAMON
Yes.

Yes.

ARCITE
Am not I liable to those affections,
Those joys, griefs, angers, fears, my friend shall suffer?

*Do I not suffer the same feelings my friend does,
sharing his joys, griefs, angers and fears?*

PALAMON
Ye may be.

You might.

ARCITE
Why then would you deal so cunningly,
So strangely, so unlike a noble kinsman,
To love alone? Speak truly: do you think me
Unworthy of her sight?

*Then why would you be so devious,
so crooked, so unlike a noble kinsman,
to love without me? Tell the truth: do you think
I shouldn't be allowed to look at her?*

PALAMON
No; but unjust
If thou pursue that sight.

*No; but you would be wrong
to do more than that.*

ARCITE
Because another
First sees the enemy, shall I stand still,
And let mine honor down, and never charge?

*Because someone else
saw the enemy first, should I stand still,
never charging, disgracing myself?*

PALAMON
Yes, if he be but one.

Yes, if there is only one enemy.

ARCITE
But say that one
Had rather combat me?

*But what if that one
would sooner fight me?*

PALAMON
Let that one say so,
And use thy freedom; else, if thou pursuest her,
Be as that cursed man that hates his country,
A branded villain.

*Let that one say so,
then you can act freely; otherwise, if you chase
her, you will be as bad as a traitor to his
country, branded as a villain.*

ARCITE

You are mad.

PALAMON
I must be—
Till thou art worthy, Arcite, it concerns me,
And in this madness if I hazard thee
And take thy life, I deal but truly.

ARCITE
Fie, sir!
You play the child extremely. I will love her,
I must, I ought to do so, and I dare—
And all this justly.

PALAMON
O that now, that now
Thy false-self and thy friend had but this fortune
To be one hour at liberty, and grasp
Our good swords in our hands, I would quickly teach thee
What 'twere to filch affection from another!
Thou art baser in it than a cutpurse.
Put but thy head out of this window more,
And as I have a soul, I'll nail thy life to't!

ARCITE
Thou dar'st not, fool, thou canst not, thou art feeble.
Put my head out? I'll throw my body out,
And leap the garden, when I see her next,
And pitch between her arms to anger thee.

PALAMON
No more; the keeper's coming. I shall live
To knock thy brains out with my shackles.

ARCITE
Do.

JAILER
By your leave, gentlemen.

PALAMON
Now, honest keeper?

You are mad.

I need to be–
until you are deserving of her, Arcite, it concerns me, and if in this madness I risk you and it cost you your life, I would only be doing the right thing.

Damn you, sir!
You are like a child. I will love her, I must, I ought to, and I dare to– and this is all permissible.

Oh, I wish that now
your deceiving self and your friend had the luck to have an hour of freedom, holding our good swords in our hands, I will quickly show you
what it means to steal someone else's love! You are worse than a pickpocket.
If you put your head out of this window just once more
I swear to heaven that I'll kill you for it!

You wouldn't dare, fool, you can't, you are weak.
Put my head out? I'll throw my body out, and leap into the garden, next time I see her, and jump into her arms to anger you.

Enter Jailer above.

Enough of that; the jailer's coming. I shall live long enough to bash your brains out with my chains.

Do.

Excuse me, gentlemen.

What is it, good jailer?

JAILER
Lord Arcite, you must presently to th' Duke;
The cause I know not yet.

*Lord Arcite, you must go to the Duke at once;
I don't know the reason for it.*

ARCITE
I am ready, keeper.

I am ready, jailer.

JAILER
Prince Palamon, I must awhile bereave you
Of your fair cousin's company.

*Prince Palamon, I must deprive you of your
fair cousin's company for a while.*

Exeunt Arcite and Jailer.

PALAMON
And me too,
Even when you please, of life. Why is he sent
for?
It may be he shall marry her; he's goodly,
And like enough the Duke hath taken notice
Both of his blood and body. But his falsehood!
Why should a friend be treacherous? If that
Get him a wife so noble and so fair,
Let honest men ne'er love again. Once more
I would but see this fair one. Blessed garden,
And fruit and flowers more blessed, that still
blossom
As her bright eyes shine on ye, would I were,
For all the fortune of my life hereafter,
Yon little tree, yon blooming apricock!
How I would spread, and fling my wanton arms
In at her window! I would bring her fruit
Fit for the gods to feed on; youth and pleasure,
Still as she tasted, should be doubled on her,
And if she be not heavenly, I would make her
So near the gods in nature, they should fear her;
And then I am sure she would love me.

*And you can deprive me
of my life if you like. Why has he been sent for?
It may be that he will marry her; he is
handsome,
and I expect the Duke has taken notice
of his breeding and his body. But his treachery!
Why would a friend be treacherous? If that
gets him such a noble and beautiful wife,
then honest men should never love. I want to
see this beautiful one once more. Blessed
garden, and the fruit and flowers are more
blessed, blossoming
as her bright eyes shine on you, I would
exchange everything I will get in my life from
now on just to be that little tree, that flowering
apricot! How I would spread, and throw my
lustful arms in through her windows! I would
bring her fruit fit for the gods; as she tasted
them youth and pleasure would be doubled for
her, and if she is not divine, I would make her
so close to the gods in nature that they would
fear her; and then I am sure she would love me.*

Enter Jailer above.

How now, keeper,
Where's Arcite?

*Hello there, jailer,
where is Arcite?*

JAILER
Banish'd. Prince Pirithous
Obtained his liberty; but never more,
Upon his oath and life, must he set foot
Upon this kingdom.

*Exiled. Prince Pirithous
won his freedom; but he has had to swear
on his life that he will not set foot
in this kingdom.*

PALAMON
He's a blessed man!
He shall see Thebes again, and call to arms
The bold young men that when he bids 'em charge,
Fall on like fire. Arcite shall have a fortune,
If he dare make himself a worthy lover,
Yet in the field to strike a battle for her;
And if he lose her then, he's a cold coward.
How bravely may he bear himself to win her,
If he be noble Arcite—thousand ways!
Were I at liberty, I would do things
Of such a virtuous greatness that this lady,
This blushing virgin, should take manhood to her
And seek to ravish me.

JAILER
My lord, for you
I have this charge too—

PALAMON
To discharge my life?

JAILER
No, but from this place to remove your lordship;
The windows are too open.

PALAMON
Devils take 'em
That are so envious to me! Prithee kill me.

JAILER
And hang for't afterward!

PALAMON
By this good light,
Had I a sword, I would kill thee.

JAILER
Why, my lord?

PALAMON
Thou bring'st such pelting scurvy news continually,

Aside.
He's a lucky man!
He shall see Thebes again, and challenge
the bold young men who will fall on him like fire
when he tells them to charge. Arcite will be
lucky, if he dares to make himself a worthy
lover, to take to the field to fight for her;
and if he loses her then, he's a cold-blooded coward.
How bravely he could act to win her,
if he is noble Arcite–there are a thousand ways!
If I was free, I would do things
so virtuous and so great that this lady,
this blushing virgin, would become like a man
and try to rape me.

My lord, I have a duty
to do for you as well–

To take my life?

No, but to take your lordship from this place;
the windows are not secure.

Damn those
who are so spiteful to me! Please kill me.

And hang for it afterwards!

I swear by the sun,
if I had a sword, I would kill you.

Why, my lord?

You're always bringing such petty wretched news,

Thou art not worthy life. I will not go.

you don't deserve life. I will not go.

JAILER
Indeed you must, my lord.

You have to, my lord.

PALAMON
May I see the garden?

May I see the garden?

JAILER
No.

No.

PALAMON
Then I am resolv'd, I will not go.

Then I have decided, I won't go.

JAILER
I must
Constrain you then; and for you are dangerous
I'll clap more irons on you.

*I shall
how to force you then; and as you are
dangerous, I will put more chains on you.*

PALAMON
Do, good keeper.
I'll shake 'em so, ye shall not sleep,
I'll make ye a new morris. Must I go?

*Do so, good jailer.
I'll rattle them so much, you won't get any
sleep, I'll be like a Morris dancer. Must I go?*

JAILER
There is no remedy.

There's nothing for it.

PALAMON
Farewell, kind window.
May rude wind never hurt thee! O my lady,
If ever thou hast felt what sorrow was,
Dream how I suffer!—Come; now bury me.

*Aside.
Goodbye, kind window.
May the rough winds never hurt you! Oh my
lady, if you ever felt what sorrow was,
dream of how I suffer!–Come; bury me.*

Exeunt Palamon and Jailer.

Scene III

The country near Athens.

(Arcite, Four Country People)

Enter Arcite.

ARCITE
Banish'd the kingdom? 'Tis a benefit,
A mercy I must thank 'em for; but banish'd
The free enjoying of that face I die for—
O, 'twas a studied punishment, a death
Beyond imagination! Such a vengeance
That were I old and wicked, all my sins
Could never pluck upon me. Palamon!
Thou hast the start now; thou shalt stay and see
Her bright eyes break each morning 'gainst thy
window,
And let in life into thee; thou shalt feed
Upon the sweetness of a noble beauty,
That nature nev'r exceeded, nor nev'r shall.
Good gods! What happiness has Palamon!
Twenty to one, he'll come to speak to her,
And if she be as gentle as she's fair,
I know she's his; he has a tongue will tame
tempests,
And make the wild rocks wanton. Come what
can come,
The worst is death: I will not leave the
kingdom.
I know mine own is but a heap of ruins,
And no redress there. If I go, he has her.
I am resolv'd another shape shall make me,
Or end my fortunes. Either way, I am happy:
I'll see her, and be near her, or no more.

Banished from the kingdom? It's a good thing,
a mercy I must thank them for; but I have been
banished from freely enjoying the face that I
would die for– oh, it was a clever punishment, a
fate worse than death! If I were old and wicked,
all my sins could never bring down such a
punishment upon me. Palamon!
You have got a head start; you can stay and see
her bright eyes every morning through your
window,
giving life to you; you will feed
on the sweetness of her noble beauty,
the greatest work of nature there will ever be.
Good gods! What happiness Palamon has!
twenty to one that he will get to speak to her,
and if she is as kind as she is beautiful,
I know he'll win her; he has a tongue which can
calm storms,
and make the wild rocks lustful. Bring on
whatever will happen,
death is the worst thing I have to fear: I will not
leave the kingdom.
I know my kingdom is just a heap of ruins,
there's nothing for me there. If I leave, he will
have her. I have decided that things will have to
go differently or I will end my life. Either way, I
will be happy: I will see her, and be near her,
or I won't be alive.

Retires.

Enter four Country People, and one with a garland before them.
FIRST COUNTRY FOLK

54

My masters, I'll be there, that's certain.

My masters, I'll be there, I promise.
SECOND COUNTRY FOLK
And I'll be there.

THIRD COUNTRY FOLK
And I.

FOURTH COUNTRY FOLK
Why then have with ye, boys! 'Tis but a
chiding.
Let the plough play today, I'll tickle't out
Of the jades' tails tomorrow.

FIRST COUNTRY FOLK
I am sure
To have my wife as jealous as a turkey.
But that's all one, I'll go through, let her
mumble.

SECOND COUNTRY FOLK
Clap her aboard tomorrow night, and stow her,
And all's made up again.

THIRD COUNTRY FOLK
Ay, do but put
A fescue in her fist, and you shall see her
Take a new lesson out, and be a good wench.
Do we all hold against the Maying?

FOURTH COUNTRY FOLK
Hold?
What should ail us?

THIRD COUNTRY FOLK
Arcas will be there.

SECOND COUNTRY FOLK
And Sennois,
And Rycas, and three better lads nev'r danc'd
Under green tree; and ye know what wenches,
ha?
But will the dainty domine, the schoolmaster,
Keep touch, do you think? For he does all, ye
know.

THIRD COUNTRY FOLK
He'll eat a horn-book ere he fail. Go to!

I'll be there too.

And me.

Well then I'll come with you, boys! I'll only get a telling off.
I'll leave the plough idle today, I'll whip the nags unmercifully tomorrow.

I am sure
my wife will be as jealous as a turkey.
But that doesn't matter, I'll do it, let her grumble.

Jump on board her tomorrow night, fill her up, and everything will be all right again.

Yes, just put
a rod in her fist, and you will see her learn a new lesson, and behave herself.
Are we all determined to go to the May Day Festival?

Determined?
What is there to stop us?

Arcas will be there.

And Sennois,
and Rycas, and three better lads never danced under the maypole; and you know what girls there will be, eh?
But will that refined schoolmaster, come up to scratch, do you think? For he organises everything, you know.

He'd eat a textbook before he let us down.

The matter's too far driven between him
And the tanner's daughter to let slip now;
And she must see the Duke, and she must dance
too.

Come on! The business between him and the
tanner's daughter is too far gone for him to
back out now;
and she must see the Duke, and she must dance.

FOURTH COUNTRY FOLK
Shall we be lusty?

Shall we be lusty?

SECOND COUNTRY FOLK
All the boys in Athens
Blow wind i' th' breech on 's, and here I'll be,
And there I'll be, for our town, and here again,
And there again. Ha, boys, heigh for the
weavers!

We'll leave all the boys in Athens
puffing in our wake, and I'll be here,
then I'll be there, for our town, and here again,
and there again. Come on boys, hurray for the
weavers!

FIRST COUNTRY FOLK
This must be done i' th' woods.

We must do this in the woods.

FOURTH COUNTRY FOLK
O, pardon me!

Oh, excuse me!

SECOND COUNTRY FOLK
By any means; our thing of learning says so—
Where he himself will edify the Duke
Most parlously in our behalfs. He's excellent i'
th' woods,
Bring him to th' plains, his learning makes no
cry.

This is the way; our educated man says so—
he himself will instruct the Duke energetically
on our behalf.
He is excellent in the woods,
bring him to the open country and he doesn't
make a sound.

THIRD COUNTRY FOLK
We'll see the sports, then every man to 's
tackle!
And, sweet companions, let's rehearse by any
means
Before the ladies see us, and do sweetly,
And God knows what may come on't.

We'll watch the games, then every man should
look to his equipment!
And, sweet friends, let's find any way we can
rehearse
before the ladies see us, and if we do it well,
God knows what good it might do us.

FOURTH COUNTRY FOLK
Content. The sports
Once ended, we'll perform. Away, boys, and
hold!

I agree. Once the sports
are over, we'll do our bit. Off we go, boys, and
stick together!

ARCITE
By your leaves, honest friends: pray you,
whither go you?

Comes forward.
If you'll excuse me, honest friends: may I ask
where you are going?

FOURTH COUNTRY FOLK
Whither? Why, what a question's that?

Where? Why, what sort of question is that?

ARCITE
Yes, 'tis a question
To me that know not.

Well, it's a question
asked by me who doesn't know the answer.

THIRD COUNTRY FOLK
To the games, my friend.

We're going to the games, my friend.

SECOND COUNTRY FOLK
Where were you bred you know it not?

Where were you born to not know that?

ARCITE
Not far, sir.
Are there such games today?

Not far away, sir.
Are they holding these games today?

FIRST COUNTRY FOLK
Yes, marry, are there;
And such as you never saw. The Duke himself
Will be in person there.

They certainly are;
games the like of which you've never seen. The
Duke himself will be there in person.

ARCITE
What pastimes are they?

What sort of things do they do?

SECOND COUNTRY FOLK
Wrastling and running.—'Tis a pretty fellow.

Wrestling and running.–This is a funny chap.

THIRD COUNTRY FOLK
Thou wilt not go along?

Won't you come along?

ARCITE
Not yet, sir.

Not yet, sir.

FOURTH COUNTRY FOLK
Well, sir,
Take your own time. Come, boys.

Well, sir,
take your own time. Come, boys.

FIRST COUNTRY FOLK
My mind misgives me
This fellow has a veng'ance trick o' th' hip,
Mark how his body's made for't.

I'm a bit worried,
this chap looks as though he could be a very
good dancer,
see how his body looks as if he's made for it.

SECOND COUNTRY FOLK
I'll be hang'd though
If he dare venture. Hang him, plum porridge!

I'll be hanged
if he dares to turn up. Hang him, great

He wrastle? He roast eggs! Come let's be gone, lads.

ARCITE
This is an offer'd opportunity
I durst not wish for. Well I could have wrestled,
The best men call'd it excellent; and run
Swifter than wind upon a field of corn,
Curling the wealthy ears, never flew. I'll venture,
And in some poor disguise be there. Who knows
Whether my brows may not be girt with garlands,
And happiness prefer me to a place
Where I may ever dwell in sight of her?

lumberer! Him wrestle? As likely as him roasting eggs! Come on, let's go lads.

Exeunt four Countrymen.

*This is a better chance
and I could have hoped for. I used to be a good wrestler,
the experts said I was excellent; and I can run faster than any wind that ever rustled
through a field of corn. I'll risk it,
and go there disguised as a poor man. Who knows,
I might win some prizes there and so be given a position through my success where I could live for ever in sight of her.*

Exit Arcite.

Scene IV

Athens. A room in the prison.

(Jailer's Daughter)

Enter Jailer's Daughter alone.

JAILER'S DAUGHTER
Why should I love this gentleman? 'Tis odds
He never will affect me. I am base,
My father the mean keeper of his prison,
And he a prince. To marry him is hopeless;
To be his whore is witless. Out upon't!
What pushes are we wenches driven to
When fifteen once has found us! First, I saw
him:
I, seeing, thought he was a goodly man;
He has as much to please a woman in him
(If he please to bestow it so) as ever
These eyes yet look'd on. Next, I pitied him;
And so would any young wench o' my
conscience
That ever dream'd, or vow'd her maidenhead
To a young handsome man. Then, I lov'd him,
Extremely lov'd him, infinitely lov'd him;
And yet he had a cousin, fair as he too;
But in my heart was Palamon, and there,
Lord, what a coil he keeps! To hear him
Sing in an evening, what a heaven it is!
And yet his songs are sad ones. Fairer spoken
Was never gentleman. When I come in
To bring him water in a morning, first
He bows his noble body, then salutes me thus:
"Fair gentle maid, good morrow. May thy
goodness
Get thee a happy husband!" Once he kiss'd
me—
I lov'd my lips the better ten days after.
Would he would do so ev'ry day! He grieves
much,
And me as much to see his misery.

What should I do to make him know I love him,
For I would fain enjoy him? Say I ventur'd

*Why do I love this gentleman? The odds are
that he will never love me. I am lowborn,
my father is the mean jailer of his prison,
and he is a prince. There's no hope of marrying
him, and I would be an idiot to be his whore.
Dammit!
What lengths we girls are driven to
once we have turned fifteen! First, I saw him:
when I saw him I thought he was a handsome
man; he has as much good stuff to please a
woman, if he ever chooses to share it, as these
eyes ever saw. Next, I pitied him;
that's what any young girl would do if she
had ever dreamed, or promised her virginity
to a handsome young man. Then, I loved him,
loved him hugely, infinitely;
but he had a cousin, just as handsome;
but my heart had fallen for Palamon, and there,
lord, what a disturbance he causes! Hearing
him
sing in the evening, how heavenly that is!
And yet his songs are sad. No gentleman
was ever so kindly spoken. When I come in
to bring him water in the morning, he first
bows to me, then he greets me in this way:
"Beautiful kind maid, good day. May your
goodness
bring you a happy marriage!" He once kissed
me–*

I liked my lips so much more for the next ten
days. I wish he would do that every day! He is
often depressed
and I'm just as depressed to see his misery.
What can I do to let him know I love him,
that I would like to have him? What if I risked

To set him free? What says the law then?
Thus much for law or kindred! I will do it,
And this night, or tomorrow, he shall love me.

*setting him free? What would the law say then?
I don't care about law or family! I will do it,
and tonight, or tomorrow, he will love me.*

Exit.

Scene V

Athens. An open place.

(Theseus, Hippolyta, Pirithous, Emilia, Arcite)

This short flourish of cornets, and shouts within. Enter Theseus, Hippolyta, Pirithous, Emilia, Arcite disguised, with a garland, etc.

THESEUS
You have done worthily. I have not seen,
Since Hercules, a man of tougher sinews.
What e'er you are, you run the best, and wrastle,
That these times can allow.

ARCITE
I am proud to please you.

THESEUS
What country bred you?

ARCITE
This; but far off, prince.

THESEUS
Are you a gentleman?

ARCITE
My father said so;
And to those gentle uses gave me life.

THESEUS
Are you his heir?

ARCITE
His youngest, sir.

THESEUS
Your father
Sure is a happy sire then. What proves you?

ARCITE
A little of all noble qualities:

You did very well. I have not seen,
since Hercules, a man with better muscles.
Whoever you are, you are the best runner, and
wrestler,
that we have seen in these times.

I am happy that you are pleased with me.

What country did you grow up in?

This one; but a long way off, prince.

Are you a gentleman?

My father said so;
and he raised me as one.

Are you his heir?

I am his youngest, sir.

Your father
certainly is a lucky one then. What shows you
are a gentleman?

I have a little of all the noble qualities:

I could have kept a hawk, and well have hollow'd
To a deep cry of dogs; I dare not praise
My feat in horsemanship, yet they that knew me
Would say it was my best piece; last, and greatest,
I would be thought a soldier.

I can hunt with a hawk, and have ridden with hounds; I dare not praise my achievements in horsemanship, but those who know me said it was my best accomplishment; lastly, and most important, I want to be thought of as a soldier.

THESEUS
You are perfect.

You are perfect.

PIRITHOUS
Upon my soul, a proper man!

I swear, a real man!

EMILIA
He is so.

He certainly is.

PIRITHOUS
How do you like him, lady?

What do you think of him, lady?

HIPPOLYTA
I admire him;
I have not seen so young a man so noble
(If he say true) of his sort.

*I admire him;
I have never seen such a young man
(if he's telling the truth) so noble.*

EMILIA
Believe
His mother was a wondrous handsome woman,
His face, methinks, goes that way.

*I imagine
his mother was a very beautiful woman,
I think his face shows that.*

HIPPOLYTA
But his body
And fiery mind illustrate a brave father.

*But his body
and passionate mind show he had a brave father.*

PIRITHOUS
Mark how his virtue, like a hidden sun,
Breaks through his baser garments.

See how his virtue, like the sun behind clouds, shows through his poor clothes.

HIPPOLYTA
He's well got sure.

He's certainly well bred.

THESEUS
What made you seek this place, sir?

What made you come to this place, sir?

ARCITE

Noble Theseus,
To purchase name, and do my ablest service
To such a well-found wonder as thy worth,
For only in thy court, of all the world,
Dwells fair-ey'd honor.

PIRITHOUS
All his words are worthy.

THESEUS
Sir, we are much indebted to your travel,
Nor shall you lose your wish. Pirithous,
Dispose of this fair gentleman.

PIRITHOUS
Thanks, Theseus.—
What e'er you are, y' are mine, and I shall give
you
To a most noble service—to this lady,
This bright young virgin. Pray observe her
goodness.
You have honor'd her fair birthday with your
virtues,
And as your due y' are hers. Kiss her fair hand,
sir.

ARCITE
Sir, y' are a noble giver. Dearest beauty,
Thus let me seal my vow'd faith.

When your servant
(Your most unworthy creature) but offends you,
Command him die, he shall.

EMILIA
That were too cruel.
If you deserve well, sir, I shall soon see't.
Y' are mine, and somewhat better than your
rank I'll use you.

PIRITHOUS
I'll see you furnish'd, and because you say
You are a horseman, I must needs entreat you
This afternoon to ride, but 'tis a rough one.

Noble Theseus,
to win fame, and to offer my best service
to such a great man as you,
for it's only in your court, out of all the world,
where glorious honour can be found.

Everything he says is good.

Sir, we appreciate your coming here,
and you shall get what you wish. Pirithous,
make arrangements for this fine gentleman.

Thanks, Theseus—
whatever you are, you are mine, and I will put
you
to a very noble task—I'll give you to this lady,
this bright young virgin. Please look at her
goodness.
Your performance has honoured her birthday,
and so you deserve to be hers. Kiss her lovely
hand, sir.

Sir, you give generously. Dearest beauty,
please let me put the seal on my oath to you.

Kisses Emilia's hand.

When your servant,
your most unworthy creature, upsets you,
if you tell him to die, he will.

That would be too cruel.
If you deserve good treatment, sir, I will soon
know. You are mine, and I'll treat you rather
better than your rank deserves.

I'll see that you are kitted out, and because you
say you are a horseman, I'd like to invite you
to come riding this afternoon, but it is a rough

ARCITE

I like him better, prince, I shall not then
Freeze in my saddle.

*I prefer that, prince, I don't like
just sitting in my saddle.*

THESEUS

Sweet, you must be ready,
And you, Emilia, and you, friend, and all,
Tomorrow, by the sun, to do observance
To flow'ry May, in Dian's wood. Wait well,
sir,
Upon your mistress. Emily, I hope
He shall not go afoot.

ride.

*Darling, you must be ready,
and you, Emilia, and you, friend, and everyone,
tomorrow, at sunrise, to worship
the flowery May, in Diana's woods. Serve your
mistress
well, sir. Emilia, I hope
he won't be walking.*

EMILIA

That were a shame, sir,
While I have horses.—Take your choice, and
what
You want at any time, let me but know it.
If you serve faithfully, I dare assure you
You'll find a loving mistress.

*That would be wrong, sir,
while I have horses.–Choose what you want,
and any time you need anything just let me
know.
If you serve me faithfully, I can promise you
you will find I am a loving mistress.*

ARCITE

If I do not,
Let me find that my father ever hated,
Disgrace and blows.

*If I don't
I hope I will get what my father always hated,
disgrace and beatings.*

THESEUS

Go lead the way; you have won it.
It shall be so; you shall receive all dues
Fit for the honor you have won; 'twere wrong
else.
Sister, beshrew my heart, you have a servant
That if I were a woman, would be master,
But you are wise.

*You lead the way; you've won the right.
This is how it will be; you will get everything
you deserve for your performance; that's only
right.
Sister, I swear, you have a servant
who, if I were a woman, would be my master;
but you are wise.*

EMILIA

I hope too wise for that, sir.

Too wise for that, I hope, sir.

Flourish. Exeunt omnes.

Scene VI

Athens. Before the prison.
(Jailer's Daughter)

Enter Jailer's Daughter alone.

JAILER'S DAUGHTER
Let all the dukes and all the devils roar,
He is at liberty! I have ventur'd for him,
And out I have brought him to a little wood
A mile hence. I have sent him where a cedar,
Higher than all the rest, spreads like a plane
Fast by a brook, and there he shall keep close
Till I provide him files and food, for yet
His iron bracelets are not off. O Love,
What a stout-hearted child thou art! My father
Durst better have endur'd cold iron than done
it.
I love him beyond love and beyond reason,
Or wit, or safety. I have made him know it.
I care not, I am desperate. If the law
Find me, and then condemn me for't, some
wenches,
Some honest-hearted maids, will sing my dirge,
And tell to memory my death was noble,
Dying almost a martyr. That way he takes
I purpose is my way too. Sure he cannot
Be so unmanly as to leave me here.
If he do, maids will not so easily
Trust men again. And yet he has not thank'd
me
For what I have done; no, not so much as kiss'd
me;
And that, methinks, is not so well; nor scarcely
Could I persuade him to become a freeman,
He made such scruples of the wrong he did
To me and to my father. Yet I hope,
When he considers more, this love of mine
Will take more root within him. Let him do
What he will with me, so he use me kindly,
For use me so he shall, or I'll proclaim him,
And to his face, no man. I'll presently
Provide him necessaries, and pack my clothes

Let all the Dukes and all the devils roar,
he is free! I have risked it for him,
and I have brought him out to a little wood
a mile away. I have put him where a cedar,
the highest tree around, spreads like a plane
right next to a stream, and he will stay there
until I can bring him food and a file, for he still
has his iron chains on. Oh love,
what a strong child you are! My father
would rather have been stabbed than do it.
I love him more than love, reason,
sense or safety. I have told him so.
I don't care, I'm desperate. If the law
finds me, and sentences me for it, some girls,
some honest hearted maids, will sing my
funeral song,
and tell history that my death was noble,
that I almost died as a martyr. Wherever he
goes
I shall follow. He surely can't be so
ungentlemanly as to leave me here.
If he does, girls will not trust men
so easily again. But he hasn't thanked me
for what I've done; no, he hasn't even kissed
me;
and that, I think, is not a good sign; I could
hardly
persuade him to take his freedom,
he made such a fuss about the harm he was
doing
me and my father. But I hope,
when he thinks about it more, he will start
to appreciate my love for him. He can do
what he wants with me, as long as he has me,
and have me he will, or I will declare him,
to his face, no man. I'll soon

up,
And where there is a path of ground I'll
venture,
So he be with me. By him, like a shadow,
I'll ever dwell. Within this hour the whoobub
Will be all o'er the prison. I am then
Kissing the man they look for. Farewell, father;
Get many more such prisoners and such
daughters,
And shortly you may keep yourself. Now to
him!

*bring him what he needs, and pack up my
clothes, and wherever the path goes I will
follow, as long as he is with me. I will stick to
him like a shadow. Within the hour the alarm
will be raised all over the prison. By then I will
be kissing the man they search for. Farewell,
father;*

*if you have many more prisoners and daughters
like this,
you'll soon have to lock yourself up. Now I must
go to him!*

Exit.

Act III

Scene I

A forest near Athens.

(Arcite, Palamon)

Cornets in sundry places. Noise and hallowing, as people a-Maying. Enter Arcite alone.

ARCITE

The Duke has lost Hippolyta; each took	*The Duke has parted from Hippolyta; each one*
A several land. This is a solemn rite	*gone to a different area. This is a solemn duty*
They owe bloom'd May, and the Athenians pay it	*they perform for blooming May, and the Athenians*
To th' heart of ceremony. O queen Emilia,	*place it at the heart of their ceremony. O Queen*
Fresher than May, sweeter	*Emilia, fresher than May, sweeter*
Than her gold buttons on the boughs, or all	*than the buds on the branches, or all*
Th' enamell'd knacks o' th' mead or garden! Yea	*the painted ornaments of fields and gardens! Yes,*
(We challenge too) the bank of any nymph,	*I say you're better than any nymph's riverbank*
That makes the stream seem flowers! Thou, O jewel	*which makes the stream seem as though it's made of flowers!*
O' th' wood, o' th' world, hast likewise blest a place	*You jewel of the woods, of the world, you bless a place in the same way*
With thy sole presence. In thy rumination	*just by being there. I hope that as you reflect*
That I, poor man, might eftsoons come between	*that a poor man like me could occasionally come to mind*
And chop on some cold thought! Thrice-blessed chance,	*and interrupt your thoughts! It would be greatly blessed chance,*
To drop on such a mistress, expectation	*to land on such a mistress, there's no shame in*
Most guiltless on't. Tell me, O Lady Fortune	*hoping for it. Tell me, O Lady Fortune*
(Next after Emily my sovereign), how far	*(my Queen apart from Emily), how much*
I may be proud. She takes strong note of me,	*I can be proud. She takes much notice of me,*
Hath made me near her; and this beauteous morn	*keeps me near her; and this lovely morning*
(The prim'st of all the year) presents me with	*(the best of the whole year) she gave me*
A brace of horses; two such steeds might well	*a pair of horses; a pair that might well carry*
Be by a pair of kings back'd, in a field	*a pair of Kings, as they battled each other*
That their crowns' titles tried. Alas, alas,	*for their crowns. Alas, alas,*
Poor cousin Palamon, poor prisoner, thou	*Poor cousin Palamon, poor prisoner, you*
So little dream'st upon my fortune that	*never dreamed that I would have such luck,*
Thou think'st thyself the happier thing to be	*you think that you are more fortunate, being*
So near Emilia. Me thou deem'st at Thebes,	*so close to Emilia. You think I am at Thebes,*
And therein wretched, although free. But if	*and miserable there, even though free. But if*
Thou knew'st my mistress breath'd on me, and that	*you knew my mistress was talking to me, and that*

I ear'd her language, liv'd in her eye, O coz,
What passion would enclose thee!

*I was listening to her words, being seen by her,
how furious you would be!*

Enter Palamon, as out of a bush, with his shackles; bends his fist at Arcite.

PALAMON
Traitor kinsman,
Thou shouldst perceive my passion, if these signs
Of prisonment were off me, and this hand
But owner of a sword! By all oaths in one,
I, and the justice of my love, would make thee
A confess'd traitor! O thou most perfidious
That ever gently look'd! The void'st of honor
That ev'r bore gentle token! Falsest cousin
That ever blood made kin, call'st thou her thine?
I'll prove it in my shackles, with these hands
Void of appointment, that thou li'st, and art
A very thief in love, a chaffy lord,
Nor worth the name of villain! Had I a sword,
And these house-clogs away—

*You treacherous kinsman,
you would feel my anger, if I wasn't wearing
the shackles, and my hand
was holding a sword! I swear by everything
that I, and my true love, would make you
confess your treachery! You are the most
unfaithful man that ever looked kind! The most
dishonourable that ever pretended otherwise!
You are the most false cousin anyone was ever
related to, do you say she is yours?
Even with my chains, with these hands
which don't have a sword, I'll prove that you
are lying, and are an absolute thief in love, a
worthless lord who can't even be dignified with
the name of the villain! If I had a sword,
and could be rid of these shackles–*

ARCITE
Dear cousin Palamon—

Dear cousin Palamon–

PALAMON
Cozener Arcite, give me language such
As thou hast show'd me feat.

*You cheating Arcite, speak to me in the same
way that you have treated me.*

ARCITE
Not finding in
The circuit of my breast any gross stuff
To form me like your blazon, holds me to
This gentleness of answer: 'tis your passion
That thus mistakes, the which to you being enemy,
Cannot to me be kind. Honor and honesty
I cherish and depend on, howsoev'r
You skip them in me, and with them, fair coz,
I'll maintain my proceedings. Pray be pleas'd
To show in generous terms your griefs, since that
Your question's with your equal, who professes
To clear his own way with the mind and sword
Of a true gentleman.

*As I can't find
anything within me so bad that makes
me fit your description, I'm obliged
to give you a polite answer: it's your passion
that's making you mistaken, it's an enemy to you,
so can't be kind to me. I love and cherish
honour and honesty, however much you
say I am missing them, and I will carry on
using them, fair cousin. Please show your
grief in well mannered terms, since you
are arguing with your equal, who says
that he makes his own way with the mind and sword
of a true gentleman.*

PALAMON

That thou durst, Arcite!

How dare you do this, Arcite!

ARCITE

My coz, my coz, you have been well advertis'd
How much I dare; y'ave seen me use my sword
Against th' advice of fear. Sure, of another
You would not hear me doubted, but your silence
Should break out, though i' th' sanctuary.

My cousin, my cousin, you have seen perfectly
well how much I dare; you have seen me using
my sword
without thought of fear. You would never hear
anyone else doubting me, even if you
shouted out your doubts in church.

PALAMON

Sir,
I have seen you move in such a place which well
Might justify your manhood; you were call'd
A good knight and a bold. But the whole week's not fair
If any day it rain. Their valiant temper
Men lose when they incline to treachery,
And then they fight like compell'd bears, would fly
Were they not tied.

Sir,
I have seen you behave in such a way which
was indeed very manly; you were called
a good knight and a brave one. But you can't
say a whole week was fine
if it rained on any day. Men lose their bravery
when they turn to treachery,
and then they fight like bears who are forced to,
they would run
if they weren't tied up.

ARCITE

Kinsman, you might as well
Speak this and act it in your glass, as to
His ear which now disdains you.

Kinsman, you might as well
say these words to your mirror, as saying
them to the person who now rejects you.

PALAMON

Come up to me,
Quit me of these cold gyves, give me a sword
Though it be rusty, and the charity
Of one meal lend me; come before me then,
A good sword in thy hand, and do but say
That Emily is thine, I will forgive
The trespass thou hast done me, yea, my life
If then thou carry't, and brave souls in shades
That have died manly, which will seek of me
Some news from earth, they shall get none but this—
That thou art brave and noble.

Come here,
take these cold chains off me, give me a sword,
even if it's rusty, and be so kind as to let me
have one meal; then come to me,
with a good sword in your hand, and just say
that Emily is yours, I will forgive you
for the wrong you have done me, even for
taking my life if you can manage it, and brave
souls in the underworld
that have died manly deaths, when they ask me
for news from Earth all I will tell them is that
you are brave and noble.

ARCITE

Be content,
Again betake you to your hawthorn house.

Calm yourself,
go back into your hawthorn bush.

With counsel of the night, I will be here
With wholesome viands; these impediments
Will I file off; you shall have garments, and
Perfumes to kill the smell o' th' prison; after,
When you shall stretch yourself, and say but,
"Arcite,
I am in plight," there shall be at your choice
Both sword and armor.

PALAMON
O you heavens, dares any
So noble bear a guilty business? None
But only Arcite; therefore none but Arcite
In this kind is so bold.

ARCITE
Sweet Palamon—

PALAMON
I do embrace you and your offer. For
Your offer do't I only, sir; your person
Without hypocrisy I may not wish
More than my sword's edge on't.

ARCITE
You hear the horns:
Enter your musit, lest this match between 's
Be cross'd ere met. Give me your hand,
farewell.
I'll bring you every needful thing. I pray you
Take comfort and be strong.

PALAMON
Pray hold your promise;
And do the deed with a bent brow. Most certain
You love me not; be rough with me, and pour
This oil out of your language. By this air,
I could for each word give a cuff, my stomach
Not reconcil'd by reason.

ARCITE
Plainly spoken,
Yet pardon me hard language. When I spur
My horse, I chide him not; content and anger

Under cover of night, I will come here
with good food; I shall file off
your chains; I will bring you clothes, and
perfume is to drown the smell of the prison;
after that,
when you have stretched yourself, and told me
that you are feeling better, you shall be
provided with both sword and armour.

Oh you heavens, is there anyone who's guilty
who can look so noble? Nobody
except for Arcite; and so there's nobody but
Arcite who can be as bold as this.

Sweet Palamon–

I embrace you and your offer. I'm
only doing it for your offer, sir; I would
be a hypocrite if I wished any more for your
body
than to have it beneath the edge of my sword.

Wind horns off. Cornets.

You hear the horns:
go back into your hiding place in case our
battle should be stopped before we've begun.
Give me your hand, farewell.
I'll bring you everything you need. I ask you to
be hopeful and strong.

Please keep your promise;
and do the deed with a frown. It's certain
that you don't love me; be rude to me, and
stop using this sweet language. I swear,
I could give your belt for each word, if
my anger wasn't controlled by my common
sense.

You speak plainly,
but you must allow me not to use rough
language. When I urge on my horse, I don't

In me have but one face.

Hark, sir, they call
The scatter'd to the banquet. You must guess
I have an office there.

PALAMON
Sir, your attendance
Cannot please heaven, and I know your office
Unjustly is achiev'd.

ARCITE
I've a good title.
I am persuaded this question, sick between 's,
By bleeding must be cur'd. I am a suitor
That to your sword you will bequeath this plea,
And talk of it no more.

PALAMON
But this one word:
You are going now to gaze upon my mistress,
For note you, mine she is—

ARCITE
Nay then—

PALAMON
Nay, pray you—
You talk of feeding me to breed me strength;
You are going now to look upon a sun
That strengthens what it looks on; there you have
A vantage o'er me, but enjoy't till
I may enforce my remedy. Farewell.

speak roughly to him; happiness and anger look the same in me.

Wind horns within.

Listen, sir, they are calling the scattered crowd to the banquet. You must know that I am expected there.

Sir, your attendance will not be smiled on by the gods, and I know your position has been achieved through cheating.

I have every right to be there. I see that the only way to solve the argument between us is by spilling blood. I must ask you to settle the matter with the sword, and let's have no more talking.

I'll just say this: you are now going to look at my mistress, for you must know, she is mine–

No but-

No, please– you talk of feeding me to make me strong; you are now going to look at a sun that strengthens everything it shines on; so you have an advantage over me, but enjoy it until I can make things right. Farewell.

Exeunt severally.

Scene II

Another part of the forest near Athens.

(Jailer's Daughter)

Enter Jailer's Daughter alone.

JAILER'S DAUGHTER

He has mistook the brake I meant, is gone
After his fancy. 'Tis now well-nigh morning;
No matter, would it were perpetual night,
And darkness lord o' th' world! Hark, 'tis a
wolf!
In me hath grief slain fear, and but for one
thing,
I care for nothing, and that's Palamon.
I reck not if the wolves would jaw me, so
He had this file. What if I hallow'd for him?
I cannot hallow. If I whoop'd, what then?
If he not answer'd, I should call a wolf,
And do him but that service. I have heard
Strange howls this livelong night; why may't
not be
They have made prey of him? He has no
weapons,
He cannot run, the jingling of his gyves
Might call fell things to listen, who have in
them
A sense to know a man unarm'd, and can
Smell where resistance is. I'll set it down
He's torn to pieces. They howl'd many
together,
And then they fed on him. So much for that,
Be bold to ring the bell. How stand I then?
All's char'd when he is gone. No, no, I lie:
My father's to be hang'd for his escape,
Myself to beg, if I priz'd life so much
As to deny my act, but that I would not,
Should I try death by dozens. I am mop'd:
Food took I none these two days—
Sipp'd some water. I have not clos'd mine eyes
Save when my lids scour'd off their brine. Alas,
Dissolve, my life, let not my sense unsettle

*He's mistaken the thicket I meant, he's gone
following his imagination. It's now almost
morning; it wouldn't matter if night lasted
forever, and darkness ruled the world! Listen,
it's a wolf!
Grief has killed my fear, and I only care
about one thing, and that's Palamon.
I don't care if the wolves chewed on me,
as long as he got this file. What if I shouted for
him?
I cannot shout. If I did, what would happen?
If he didn't answer, it would call a wolf,
and that would only help him. I have heard
strange howling all through the night; maybe
they have killed him? He has no weapons,
he cannot run, the jingling of his chains
might give him away to evil things, they
can sense when a man is unarmed, and can
always tell whether he can fight back. I have to
think
he's been torn to pieces. So many of them
howled together,
and then they ate him. That's the end of that,
ring the funeral bell. So where do I stand?
Everything is finished now he's gone. No, no,
I'm lying:
my father will be hanged for his escape,
I would beg for myself, if I cared enough about
life
to deny my act, but I wouldn't, even if
I had to suffer a dozen deaths. I am dizzy:*

I haven't eaten for two days–
I just sipped some water. I haven't closed my
eyes
except to blink away the tears. Alas,

Lest I should drown, or stab, or hang myself.
O state of nature, fail together in me,
Since thy best props are warp'd! So which way
now?
The best way is, the next way to a grave;
Each errant step beside is torment. Lo
The moon is down, the crickets chirp, the
screech owl
Calls in the dawn! All offices are done
Save what I fail in. But the point is this—
An end, and that is all.

let my life end, don't let me go mad
and drown, or stab, or hang, myself.
Nature, let life slip away from me,
since all that supports it is broken! Which way
now? The best way is the way to the grave;
every step that doesn't lead there is torture.
Look, the moon is set, the crickets are chirping,
the screech owl
welcomes the dawn! All jobs have been done
except mine, and I failed. In conclusion, all
I want is for everything to end.

Exit.

Scene III

Another part of the forest near Athens.

(Arcite, Palamon)

Enter Arcite with meat, wine, and files.

ARCITE
I should be near the place. Ho, cousin Palamon!

PALAMON
Arcite?

ARCITE
The same. I have brought you food and files.
Come forth and fear not, here's no Theseus.

PALAMON
Nor none so honest, Arcite.

ARCITE
That's no matter,
We'll argue that hereafter. Come, take courage,
You shall not die thus beastly. Here, sir,
drink—
I know you are faint—then I'll talk further with
you.

PALAMON
Arcite, thou mightst now poison me.

ARCITE
I might;
But I must fear you first. Sit down, and good
now
No more of these vain parleys; let us not,
Having our ancient reputation with us,
Make talk for fools and cowards. To your
health, etc.

I should be near the place. Hello, cousin
Palamon!

Enter Palamon.

Arcite?

It's me. I have brought you food and files.
Come out and don't be afraid, Theseus is not
here.

Nobody as honest as him, Arcite.

That's not important,
we'll debate that afterwards. Come, take heart,
you will not die in such horrible state. Here,
sir, drink–
I know you're faint–and then I'll talk more with
you.

Arcite, you could poison me now.

I could;
but I'd have to be frightened of you to do it. Sit
down,
and let's have no more silly talk; let's not,
bearing in mind our nobility,
talk as if we were fools and cowards. Your
good health.

Drinks.

PALAMON
Do.

Go on.

ARCITE
Pray sit down then, and let me entreat you
By all the honesty and honor in you,
No mention of this woman. 'Twill disturb us,
We shall have time enough.

*Please sit down then, and I beg you
by all the honesty and honour you have
not to mention this woman. It will set us
arguing, we have time enough for that.*

PALAMON
Well, sir, I'll pledge you.

Well, sir, I'll drink your health.

Drinks.

ARCITE
Drink a good hearty draught, it breeds good
blood, man.
Do not you feel it thaw you?

*Have a good drink, it will strengthen you, man.
Can't you feel it heating you up?*

PALAMON
Stay, I'll tell you
After a draught or two more.

*Wait, I'll tell you
after a couple more swigs.*

ARCITE
Spare it not,
The Duke has more, coz. Eat now.

*Don't stint yourself cousin,
the Duke has more. Now eat.*

PALAMON
Yes.

Yes.

Eats.

ARCITE
I am glad
You have so good a stomach.

*I'm glad
you have such a good appetite.*

PALAMON
I am gladder
I have so good meat to't.

*I'm more glad
that I have such good food to satisfy it.*

ARCITE
Is't not mad lodging
Here in the wild woods, cousin?

*Isn't it strange living
here in the wild woods, cousin?*

PALAMON
Yes, for them
That have wild consciences.

*Yes, for those
who have guilty consciences.*

ARCITE
How tastes your victuals?
Your hunger needs no sauce, I see.

PALAMON
Not much.
But if it did, yours is too tart, sweet cousin.
What is this?

ARCITE
Venison.

PALAMON
'Tis a lusty meat.
Give me more wine. Here, Arcite, to the wenches
We have known in our days! The Lord Steward's daughter—
Do you remember her?

ARCITE
After you, coz.

PALAMON
She lov'd a black-hair'd man.

ARCITE
She did so; well, sir?

PALAMON
And I have heard some call him Arcite, and—

ARCITE
Out with't, faith!

PALAMON
She met him in an arbor:
What did she there, coz? Play o' th' virginals?

ARCITE
Something she did, sir.

PALAMON
Made her groan a month for't;
Or two, or three, or ten.

How is your food?
You are hungry enough to need no sauce, I see.

Not too much.
But if I did, yours is too bitter, sweet cousin.
What is this?

Venison.

That's a strengthening meat.
Give me more wine. Here, Arcite, drink to the girls
we have known! The daughter of the Lord Steward—
do you remember her?

The same as you, cousin.

She loved a black haired man.

She did that; well, sir?

And I've heard a rumour he was called Arcite, and—

Spit it out, by God!

She met him in a leafy glade:
what did she do there, cousin? Play her piano?

She did something, sir.

She groaned for a month over it;
or two, or three, or ten.

ARCITE
The Marshal's sister
Had her share too, as I remember, cousin,
Else there be tales abroad. You'll pledge her?

*The Marshal's sister
had her share to, as I recall, cousin,
or someone's spreading untrue rumours. You
will drink to her?*

PALAMON
Yes.

Yes.

ARCITE
A pretty brown wench 'tis. There was a time
When young men went a-hunting, and a wood,
And a broad beech; and thereby hangs a tale.
Heigh-ho!

*She's a pretty brown lass. There was a time
when young men went hunting, and there was a
wood, and a broad beech tree; and there's a
story attached to that.
Hey Ho!*

PALAMON
For Emily, upon my life! Fool,
Away with this strain'd mirth! I say again,
That sigh was breath'd for Emily. Base cousin,
Dar'st thou break first?

*For Emilia, by my life! Fool,
enough of this false jollity! I tell you again,
I am sighing for Emilia. Low cousin,
are you going to be the first one to break your
promise?*

ARCITE
You are wide.

You're wide of the mark.

PALAMON
By heaven and earth,
There's nothing in thee honest.

*By heaven and earth,
there's nothing honest about you.*

ARCITE
Then I'll leave you;
You are a beast now.

*Then I'll leave you;
you are an animal to me.*

PALAMON
As thou mak'st me, traitor!

That's what you've made me, traitor!

ARCITE
There's all things needful, files and shirts and
perfumes.
I'll come again some two hours hence and
bring
That that shall quiet all.

*There are all things you need, files and shirts
and perfumes.
I'll come again two hours from now and bring
something that will end everything.*

PALAMON
A sword and armor.

A sword and armour.

ARCITE
Fear me not. You are now too foul; farewell.

Trust me. You are too foul now; farewell.

Get off your trinkets, you shall want nought.

Take off your chains, you will lack nothing.

PALAMON
Sirrah—

Sir–

ARCITE
I'll hear no more.

I'll listen to no more.

Exit.

PALAMON
If he keep touch, he dies for't.

If he comes back, he'll die for it.

Exit.

Scene IV

Another part of the forest near Athens.

(Jailer's Daughter)

Enter Jailer's Daughter.

JAILER'S DAUGHTER
I am very cold, and all the stars are out too,
The little stars and all, that look like aglets.
The sun has seen my folly. Palamon!
Alas, no; he's in heaven. Where am I now?
Yonder's the sea, and there's a ship. How't
tumbles!
And there's a rock lies watching under water;
Now, now, it beats upon it—now, now, now!
There's a leak sprung, a sound one. How they
cry!
Open her before the wind! You'll lose all else.
Up with a course or two, and tack about, boys!
Good night, good night, y' are gone. I am very
hungry:
Would I could find a fine frog! He would tell
me
News from all parts o' th' world. Then would I
make
A carreck of a cockleshell, and sail
By east and north-east to the King of Pigmies,
For he tells fortunes rarely. Now my father,
Twenty to one, is truss'd up in a trice
Tomorrow morning; I'll say never a word.
Sing.
"For I'll cut my green coat a foot above my
knee,
And I'll clip my yellow locks an inch below
mine e'e.
Hey, nonny, nonny, nonny.
He s' buy me a white cut, forth for to ride,
And I'll go seek him through the world that is
so wide.
Hey, nonny, nonny, nonny."

O for a prick now, like a nightingale,
To put my breast against! I shall sleep like a top

I am very cold, and all the stars are out too,
the little stars as well, but look like spangles.
The sun has set on my stupidity. Palamon!
Alas, no; he's in heaven. Where am I now?
There's the sea, and there's a ship. How it's
rocking!
And there's a rock lying in wait under the
water;
now, now, it's crashed against it—now, now,
now!
It's sprung a leak, a big one. How they cry!
Let her run with the wind! You'll lose
everything otherwise.
Put a sail or two up, and turn with the wind,
boys! Good night, good night, you are lost. I
am very hungry:
I wish I could find a good frog! He would tell
me news from all over the world. Then I would
make a boat out of a cockleshell, and sail
East North East to the king of pygmies,
for he is a fine fortune teller. Now my father,
almost certainly, will be hung
tomorrow morning; I'll never say a word.
[Sings]
" For I'll cut my green coat a foot above my
knees,
and I'll cut my yellow hair an inch below my
eyes.
Hey, nonny, nonny, nonny.
He's bought me a white horse, to ride out on,

and I'll go and seek him through the whole wide world.
Hey, nonny, nonny, nonny."
I wish I could drive a thorn through my chest,
like a nightingale! That way I would sleep like

else.

a top.

Exit.

Scene V

Another part of the forest near Athens.

(Schoolmaster Gerrold, Four Countrymen, Bavian, Five Wenches, Taborer, Jailer's Daughter, Theseus, Pirithous, Hippolyta, Emilia, Arcite, Dancers, Friz, Maudline, Luce, Barbary)

Enter a Schoolmaster Gerrold, four Countrymen as morris-dancers and another as the Bavian, five Wenches, with a Taborer.

GERROLD
Fie, fie,
What tediosity and disensanity
Is here among ye! Have my rudiments
Been labor'd so long with ye, milk'd unto ye,
And by a figure, even the very plum-broth
And marrow of my understanding laid upon ye,
And do you still cry, "Where?" and "How?"
and "Wherefore?"
You most coarse frieze capacities, ye jane
judgments,
Have I said, "Thus let be," and "There let be,"
And "Then let be," and no man understand me?
Pro Deum, medius fidius, ye are all dunces!
For why, here stand I; here the Duke comes;
there are you,
Close in the thicket. The Duke appears, I meet
him
And unto him I utter learned things,
And many figures; he hears, and nods, and
hums,
And then cries, "Rare!" and I go forward. At
length
I fling my cap up; mark there! Then do you,
As once did Meleager and the boar,
Break comely out before him; like true lovers,
Cast yourselves in a body decently,
And sweetly, by a figure, trace and turn, boys.

SECOND COUNTRY FOLK

FIRST COUNTRY FOLK
And sweetly we will do it, Master Gerrold.

Dammit all,
what trouble and foolishness
there is amongst you! I have
spent so long teaching you my principles,
feeding them to you, giving you
the essentials of my understanding, and you
still cry, "where?" And "how?" And "why?"
You woolly brained idiots, you coarse dullards,
have I said, "and so this is," and "there it is,"
and "and so we see," and nobody has
understood me?
Oh God, heaven help me, you are all idiots!
Look, here I am; here comes the Duke; there
you are,
hiding in the thicket. The Duke appears, I meet
him
and speak to him of intellectual matters
in many ways; he will hear me, and nod, and
hum,
and then cry, "Good!" and I will walk on.
After a while I will throw my hat up; watch out
for it!
And then you, like Meleager and the boar,
will jump out in front of him; like true lovers
you will merge your bodies together,
and dance sweetly in front of him, my boys.

And we will do it sweetly, Master Gerrold.

Draw up the company. Where's the taborer?

Gather everyone together. Where's the drummer?

THIRD COUNTRY FOLK
Why, Timothy!

Hello, Timothy!

TABORER
Here, my mad boys, have at ye!

Here, my merry boys, let's go!

GERROLD
But I say, where's their women?

Hang on, where are the women?

FOURTH COUNTRY FOLK
Here's Friz and Maudline.

Here are Friz and Maudline.

SECOND COUNTRY FOLK
And little Luce with the white legs, and
bouncing Barbary.

*And little Lucy with her white legs, and
strapping Barbara.*

FIRST COUNTRY FOLK
And freckled Nell—that never fail'd her
master.

*And freckled Nell, who never let her master
down.*

GERROLD
Where be your ribands, maids? Swim with your
bodies,
And carry it sweetly and deliverly,
And now and then a favor and a frisk.

*Where are your ribbons, girls? Glide around,
do it charmingly and lightly,
and now and then give a curtsy and a jig.*

NELL
Let us alone, sir.

You can leave it to us, sir.

GERROLD
Where's the rest o' th' music?

Where are the rest of the musicians?

THIRD COUNTRY FOLK
Dispers'd as you commanded.

They've been placed as you ordered.

GERROLD
Couple then,
And see what's wanting. Where's the Bavian?
My friend, carry your tail without offense
Or scandal to the ladies; and be sure
You tumble with audacity and manhood,
And when you bark, do it with judgment.

*Pair up then,
and will see what's missing. Where is the ape?
My friend, give us a performance that doesn't
offend or disgust the ladies; make sure you
tumble daringly and manfully, and when you
bark, do it tactfully.*

BAVIAN

Yes, sir.

GERROLD
Quo usque tandem?
 Here is a woman wanting.

FOURTH COUNTRY FOLK
We may go whistle; all the fat's i' th' fire.

GERROLD
We have, as learned authors utter, wash'd a tile,
We have been fatuus, and labored vainly.

SECOND COUNTRY FOLK
This is that scornful piece, that scurvy hilding,
That gave her promise faithfully she would
Be here, Cicely the sempster's daughter.
The next gloves that I give her shall be dogskin;
Nay, and she fail me once—You can tell,
Arcas,
She swore by wine and bread she would not
break.

GERROLD
An eel and woman,
A learned poet says, unless by th' tail
And with thy teeth thou hold, will either fail.
In manners this was false position.

FIRST COUNTRY FOLK
A fire ill take her! Does she flinch now?

THIRD COUNTRY FOLK
What
Shall we determine, sir?

GERROLD
Nothing,
Our business is become a nullity,
Yea, and a woeful and a piteous nullity.

FOURTH COUNTRY FOLK
Now when the credit of our town lay on it,
Now to be frampal, now to piss o' th' nettle!
Go thy ways, I'll remember thee, I'll fit thee!

Yes, sir.

How much longer? There's a woman missing here.

It would be a waste of time to carry on; we've blown it.

As the learned authors put it, we have laboured in vain, we have been stupid, all our work is for nothing.

It's that scornful piece, that good for nothing wretch, who faithfully promised that she would be here, Cicely the daughter of the seamstress. The next gloves I give her will be made of dog skin; no, she's let me down once–you can witness, Arcas, she swore by wine and bread that she would not let me down.

A learned poet has said that with eels and women, unless you have them by the tail with your teeth, they will both let you down. This is not a good way to behave.

May she catch a fever! Is she letting us down now?

What shall we do, sir?

Nothing, the whole thing has come to nothing, yes, a sad and useless nothing.

Now, when our town's reputation depended on it, now to be moody, to be in a bad temper! Do what you want, I'll remember this, I'll give you what you deserve!

JAILER'S DAUGHTER
"The George Alow came from the south,
From the coast of Barbary-a;
And there he met with brave gallants of war,
By one, by two, by three-a.
Well hail'd, well hail'd, you jolly gallants!
And whither now are you bound-a?
O, let me have your company
Till I come to the sound-a.
"There was three fools fell out about an howlet:
The one said it was an owl,
The other he said nay,
The third he said it was a hawk,
And her bells were cut away."

THIRD COUNTRY FOLK
There's a dainty mad woman, master,
Comes i' th' nick, as mad as a March hare.
If we can get her dance, we are made again.
I warrant her, she'll do the rarest gambols.

FIRST COUNTRY FOLK
A mad woman? We are made, boys!

GERROLD
And are you mad, good woman?

JAILER'S DAUGHTER
I would be sorry else.
Give me your hand.

GERROLD
Why?

JAILER'S DAUGHTER
I can tell your fortune.
You are a fool. Tell ten—I have pos'd him.
Buzz!
Friend, you must eat no white bread; if you do,
Your teeth will bleed extremely. Shall we
dance ho?
I know you, y' are a tinker. Sirrah tinker,
Stop no more holes but what you should.

Enter Jailer's Daughter.

Sings.
"The George Alow came from the South,
from the coast of Africa;
and there he met with strong warships,
one, two and three.
Hello, hello, you fine ships!
And where are you going?
Let me sail along with you
until I reach the harbour.
There were three fools who argued about a
young owl:
one said it was now,
the other said it wasn't,
the third said it was a hawk,
and they cut away her bells."

Here's a splendid madwoman, master,
come just in the nick of time, as mad as a
March hare. If we can get her to dance, we are
saved. I'll bet she can dance a fine jig.

A madwoman? We're saved, boys!

And are you mad, good woman?

It would be a shame otherwise.
Give me your hand.

Why?

I can tell your fortune.
You are a fool. Count to ten–that's stumped
him. Buzz!
Friend, you must not eat white bread; if you do,
your teeth will bleed terribly. Shall we dance?
I know you, you're a mender. Sir mender,
don't fill up more holes than you ought to.

GERROLD
Dii boni!
A tinker, damsel?

Good God!
A mender, girl?

JAILER'S DAUGHTER
Or a conjurer.
Raise me a devil now, and let him play
Qui passa o' th' bells and bones.

Or magician.
Summon me a devil now, and let him play
a tune on the bells and bones.

GERROLD
Go take her,
And fluently persuade her to a peace.
"Et opus exegi, quod nec Jovis ira, nec ignis"—
Strike up, and lead her in.

Take her away,
and do your best to calm her down.
"I have completed a work that neither the anger
of Jove, nor fire"– start the music, and bring
her into the dance.

SECOND COUNTRY FOLK
Come, lass, let's trip it.

Come on lass, let's dance.

JAILER'S DAUGHTER
I'll lead.

I'll lead.

THIRD COUNTRY FOLK
Do, do.

Do, do.

GERROLD
Persuasively and cunningly!

Beautifully and cleverly!

Wind horns.

Away, boys!
I hear the horns. Give me some meditation,
And mark your cue.

Off you go, boys!
I can hear the horns. Give me time to think,
and look out for your cue.

Exeunt all but Schoolmaster.

Pallas inspire me!

Pallas inspire me!

Enter Theseus, Pirithous, Hippolyta, Emilia, Arcite, and Train.

THESEUS
This way the stag took.

This is the way the stag went.

GERROLD
Stay, and edify.

Stop and learn.

THESEUS

What have we here?

PIRITHOUS

Some country sport, upon my life, sir.

THESEUS

Well, sir, go forward, we will edify.
Ladies, sit down, we'll stay it.

GERROLD

Thou doughty Duke, all hail! All hail, sweet ladies!

THESEUS

This is a cold beginning.

GERROLD

If you but favor, our country pastime made is.
We are a few of those collected here
That ruder tongues distinguish villager,
And to say verity, and not to fable,
We are a merry rout, or else a rable,
Or company, or by a figure, choris,
That 'fore thy dignity will dance a morris.
And I, that am the rectifier of all,
By title paedagogus, that let fall
The birch upon the breeches of the small ones,
And humble with a ferula the tall ones,
Do here present this machine, or this frame,
And, dainty Duke, whose doughty dismal fame
From Dis to Daedalus, from post to pillar,
Is blown abroad, help me, thy poor well-willer,
And with thy twinkling eyes look right and straight
Upon this mighty Morr—of mickle weight—
Is—now comes in, which being glu'd together
Makes Morris, and the cause that we came hither.
The body of our sport, of no small study,
I first appear, though rude, and raw, and muddy,
To speak, before thy noble Grace, this tenner;
At whose great feet I offer up my penner.
The next, the Lord of May and Lady bright,
The Chambermaid and Servingman, by night
That seek out silent hanging. Then mine Host

What's this?

I swear it must be some country entertainment, sir.

*Well, sir, carry on, we will learn.
Ladies, sit down, we'll watch.*

You good Duke, all welcomes! All welcomes, sweet ladies!

This is a dull beginning.

If you just watch, our country pastime will prosper. There are a few of us gathered here that vulgar people call villagers, and to tell the truth, and not to lie, we are merry bunch, or else we are a rabble, or a company, or metaphorically, a choir, who will dance a morris dance for your lordships. And I, who is the director of everything, a teacher by name, who whips the little ones with the birch and the bigger ones with a cane, present to you this show, this device, and, sweet Duke, whose splendid terrible fame has spread around the world to every corner, help me, you poor well-wisher, and with your twinkling eyes look clearly upon this great "moor"-meaning great weight— and then we add "is", and putting them together we make Morris, and that's why we're here. The main part of our entertainment, which isn't easy, I will show you now, though it's rough and raw and confused, let me explain what's going on to your noble grace, at his noble feat I offer my entertainment. This is the Lord of May and his bright lady, the chambermaid and serving man, who look for quiet corners at night. Then the

And his fat spouse, that welcomes to their cost
The galled traveller, and with a beck'ning
Informs the tapster to inflame the reck'ning.
Then the beast-eating Clown, and next the Fool,
The Bavian, with long tail and eke long tool,

Cum multis aliis
that make a dance.

Say "Ay," and all shall presently advance.

THESEUS
Ay, ay, by any means, dear domine.

PIRITHOUS
Produce.

GERROLD

Intrate, filii
  come forth, and foot it.

Ladies, if we have been merry,
And have pleas'd ye with a derry,
And a derry, and a down,
Say the schoolmaster's no clown.
Duke, if we have pleas'd thee too
And have done as good boys should do,
Give us but a tree or twain
For a Maypole, and again,
Ere another year run out,
We'll make thee laugh and all this rout.

THESEUS
Take twenty, domine.—How does my sweet
heart?

HIPPOLYTA
Never so pleas'd, sir.

EMILIA
'Twas an excellent dance, and for a preface,
I never heard a better.

*landlord and his fat wife, who welcome for
their profit the weary traveller, and make signs
to the barman to bump up the bill. Then there's
the beast eating clown, and then the fool, the
monkey, with a long tail and a long tool,*

*along with many others
that make up the dance.*

Give the word and we'll start at once.

Yes, yes, by all means, dear schoolmaster.

Show us.

*Knock for school.
Come in, boys,
come in and dance.
[Dance]
Enter the Dance. Music. Dance.*

*Ladies, if we have been jolly,
and have pleased you with our music,
say the schoolmaster isn't a clown.
Duke, if we have pleased you to,
and have done what good boys should do,
just give us the tree or two
to make a maypole, and again,
before another year has passed,
we'll make you laugh along with all your
company.*

*Take twenty, schoolmaster.–How is my
darling?*

I've never been so amused, sir.

*It was an excellent dance, and I never heard
a better introduction.*

THESEUS
Schoolmaster, I thank you.
One see 'em all rewarded.

PIRITHOUS
And here's something

To paint your pole withal.

THESEUS
Now to our sports again.

GERROLD
May the stag thou hunt'st stand long,
And thy dogs be swift and strong!
May they kill him without lets,
And the ladies eat his dowsets!

Come, we are all made.
Dii deaeque omnes!
Ye have danc'd rarely, wenches.

Schoolmaster, I thank you.
Somebody see they are all rewarded.

And here's something

Gives money.

to paint your pole with.

Now back to our hunting.

May the stag you're hunting wait for you,
and may your dogs be swift and strong!
May nothing get in the way of the kill,
and let the ladies eat his delicacies!

Exeunt Theseus and his company. Wind horns.

Come, we are all made.
All you gods and goddesses!
You danced beautifully, girls.

Exeunt.

Scene VI

Another part of the forest near Athens.

(Palamon, Arcite, Theseus, Hippolyta, Emilia, Pirithous)

Enter Palamon from the bush.

PALAMON
About this hour my cousin gave his faith
To visit me again, and with him bring
Two swords and two good armors. If he fail,
He's neither man nor soldier. When he left me,
I did not think a week could have restor'd
My lost strength to me, I was grown so low
And crestfall'n with my wants. I thank thee,
Arcite,
Thou art yet a fair foe; and I feel myself,
With this refreshing, able once again
To out-dure danger. To delay it longer
Would make the world think, when it comes to
hearing,
That I lay fatting like a swine, to fight,
And not a soldier: therefore this blest morning
Shall be the last; and that sword he refuses,
If it but hold, I kill him with. 'Tis justice.
So, love and fortune for me!

PALAMON

O, good morrow.

ARCITE
Good morrow, noble kinsman.

PALAMON
I have put you
To too much pains, sir.

ARCITE
That too much, fair cousin,
Is but a debt to honor, and my duty.

98

It was about this time my cousin promised
to visit me again, and bring with him
Two swords and two good suits of armour. If he
doesn't, he's neither man nor a soldier. When
he left me, I didn't think a week would have
been enough to get my strength back, I had
been laid so low by all my needs. I thank you,
Arcite, you are still a fair enemy; and now that
I am refreshed I feel that I can survive any
danger. Any further delay would make people
think, when they heard about it,
that I was a pig who preferred feasting to
fighting
and was not a soldier: so this blessed morning
shall be his last; and if that sword he offers
doesn't break, I shall kill him with it. That is
justice.
So, love and good fortune for me!

Enter Arcite with armors and swords.

Oh, good morning.

Good morning, noble kinsman.

I have given you
too much trouble, sir.

That trouble, fair cousin,
is just doing my honourable duty.

Would you were so in all, sir! I could wish ye
As kind a kinsman as you force me find
A beneficial foe, that my embraces
Might thank ye, not my blows.

ARCITE
I shall think either,
Well done, a noble recompense.

PALAMON
Then I shall quit you.

ARCITE
Defy me in these fair terms, and you show
More than a mistress to me; no more anger,
As you love any thing that's honorable.
We were not bred to talk, man. When we are
arm'd
And both upon our guards, then let our fury,
Like meeting of two tides, fly strongly from us,
And then to whom the birthright of this beauty
Truly pertains (without obbraidings, scorns,
Despisings of our persons, and such poutings,
Fitter for girls and schoolboys) will be seen,
And quickly, yours or mine. Will't please you
arm, sir?
Or if you feel yourself not fitting yet
And furnish'd with your old strength, I'll stay,
cousin,
And ev'ry day discourse you into health,
As I am spar'd. Your person I am friends with,
And I could wish I had not said I lov'd her,
Though I had died; but loving such a lady
And justifying my love, I must not fly from't.

PALAMON
Arcite, thou art so brave an enemy
That no man but thy cousin's fit to kill thee.
I am well and lusty, choose your arms.

ARCITE
Choose you, sir.

PALAMON
Wilt thou exceed in all, or dost thou do it
To make me spare thee?

---

*I wish you were like this in everything, sir! I
wish you were as good a kinsman as you are a
good enemy to me, so I could thank you with my
embraces, not my blows.*

*I would think that either,
if they are given well, would be a great reward.*

Then I shall pay you.

*Defy me in these fair terms, and you'll be like
more than a mistress to me; no more anger,
for the sake of honour.
We were not made for talking, man. When we
are armed
and both on guard, then let our anger,
like two tides meeting, be unleashed,
and then we will see who truly deserves
to have this beauty, without criticism, scorn,
name-calling and other such pouting,
more fit for girls and schoolboys,
the winner will be decided quickly. Would you
like to arm yourself, sir?
Or if you don't feel you're yet ready,
and have regained your strength, I'll wait,
cousin,
and every day I will do everything I can
to bring you back to health. I am your friend,
and I wish I hadn't said I loved her,
even if it had killed me; but loving such a lady
and having to prove my love, I can't ignore it.*

*Arcite, you are such a brave enemy
that no one but your cousin is suitable to kill
you. I am well and strong, choose your
weapons.*

You choose, sir.

*Are you going to be so fine in everything, or are
you doing it
to get me to spare you?*

ARCITE
If you think so, cousin,
You are deceived, for as I am a soldier,
I will not spare you.

If you think that, cousin,
you are deceived, for I am a soldier
and I will not spare you.

PALAMON
That's well said.

That's well said.

ARCITE
You'll find it.

You'll see the truth of it.

PALAMON
Then as I am an honest man, and love
With all the justice of affection,
I'll pay thee soundly. This I'll take.

Then as I am an honest man,
and am justified in my love,
I'll give you what you deserve. I'll take this.

ARCITE
That's mine then.
I'll arm you first.

This is mine then.
I'll put your armour on first.

PALAMON
Do. Pray thee tell me, cousin,
Where got'st thou this good armor?

Do. Please tell me, cousin,
where did you get this good armour?

ARCITE
'Tis the Duke's,
And to say true, I stole it. Do I pinch you?

It's the Duke's,
and to tell the truth, I stole it. Is that too tight?

PALAMON
No.

No.

ARCITE
Is't not too heavy?

It's not too heavy?

PALAMON
I have worn a lighter,
But I shall make it serve.

I've worn lighter,
but it will do.

ARCITE
I'll buckle't close.

I'll fix it up tight.

PALAMON
By any means.

By all means.

ARCITE
You care not for a grand-guard?

You don't want a chest protector?

PALAMON
No, no, we'll use no horses. I perceive
You would fain be at that fight.

No, no, we won't use horses. I see
you would rather fight like that.

ARCITE
I am indifferent.

I'm not bothered.

PALAMON
Faith, so am I. Good cousin, thrust the buckle
Through far enough.

Neither am I, I swear. Good cousin, push the
buckle through far enough.

ARCITE
I warrant you.

I certainly shall.

PALAMON
My casque now.

And now my helmet.

ARCITE
Will you fight bare-arm'd?

Will you fight bare armed?

PALAMON
We shall be the nimbler.

That will make us nimbler.

ARCITE
But use your gauntlets though. Those are o' th'
least;
Prithee take mine, good cousin.

But wear your gloves though. Those are the
worst pair;
please take mine, good cousin.

PALAMON
Thank you, Arcite.
How do I look? Am I fall'n much away?

Thank you, Arcite.
How do I look? Have I lost too much weight?

ARCITE
Faith, very little. Love has us'd you kindly.

I swear, very little. Love has treated you well.

PALAMON
I'll warrant thee, I'll strike home.

I promise you, I shall thrust home.

ARCITE
Do, and spare not.
I'll give you cause, sweet cousin.

Do, and don't spare me.
I'll do the same for you, sweet cousin.

PALAMON
Now to you, sir.
Methinks this armor's very like that, Arcite,
Thou wor'st that day the three kings fell, but

Now for you, sir.
This armour seems very similar to me, Arcite,
to the one you wore the day the three kings fell,

lighter.

ARCITE
That was a very good one, and that day,
I well remember, you outdid me, cousin;
I never saw such valor. When you charg'd
Upon the left wing of the enemy,
I spurr'd hard to come up, and under me
I had a right good horse.

PALAMON
You had indeed,
A bright bay, I remember.

ARCITE
Yes, but all
Was vainly labor'd in me; you outwent me,
Nor could my wishes reach you. Yet a little
I did by imitation.

PALAMON
More by virtue.
You are modest, cousin.

ARCITE
When I saw you charge first,
Methought I heard a dreadful clap of thunder
Break from the troop.

PALAMON
But still before that flew
The lightning of your valor. Stay a little;
Is not this piece too strait?

ARCITE
No, no, 'tis well.

PALAMON
I would have nothing hurt thee but my sword,
A bruise would be dishonor.

ARCITE
Now I am perfect.

PALAMON
Stand off then.

but lighter.

*That was a very good suit, and that day,
I remember it well, you beat me, cousin;
I never saw such bravery. When you charged
the enemy's left wing,
I had to gallop hard to keep up, and I had
a very good horse under me.*

*You had indeed,
a glossy bay, I remember.*

*Yes, but all
my labours were in vain; you outstripped me,
and try as I might I couldn't get to you. But I
did some good things by copying you.*

*More through your own virtue.
You are modest, cousin.*

*When I first saw you charge,
I thought I heard a terrible clap of thunder
come from the ranks of your opponents.*

*But the lightning of your bravery
preceded that. Wait a moment;
isn't this piece too tight?*

No, no, it's fine.

*I don't want anything to hurt you except my
sword, a bruise would be dishonourable.*

Now that's perfect.

Stand away then.

ARCITE
Take my sword, I hold it better.

Take my sword, I think it's the better one.

PALAMON
I thank ye. No, keep it, your life lies on it.
Here's one, if it but hold, I ask no more
For all my hopes. My cause and honor guard
me!

Thank you. No, keep it, your life depends on it.
If this one doesn't break, that's all I ask
for my purposes. May my cause and my honour
protect me!

They bow several ways; then advance and
stand.

ARCITE
And me my love!
Is there aught else to say?

And may my love protect me!
Is there anything else to say?

PALAMON
This only, and no more: thou art mine aunt's
son,
And that blood we desire to shed is mutual,
In me, thine, and in thee, mine. My sword
Is in my hand, and if thou kill'st me,
The gods and I forgive thee. If there be
A place prepar'd for those that sleep in honor,
I wish his weary soul that falls may win it.
Fight bravely, cousin. Give me thy noble hand.

Only this: you are my aunt's son,
and the blood we want to spill is shared,
I have yours in me and mine is in you. My
sword is in my hand, and if you kill me,
the gods and I will forgive you. If there is
a place set aside for the honoured dead,
I hope the weary soul of the one who falls goes
there. Fight bravely, cousin. Give me your
noble hand.

ARCITE
Here, Palamon: this hand shall never more
Come near thee with such friendship.

Here, Palamon: this is the last time this hand
will be near you in friendship.

PALAMON
I commend thee.

I praise you.

ARCITE
If I fall, curse me, and say I was a coward,
For none but such dare die in these just trials.
Once more farewell, my cousin.

If I fall, curse me, and say I was a coward,
for they are the only sort who will die in these
tests. Goodbye again, my cousin.

PALAMON
Farewell, Arcite.

Farewell, Arcite.

Fight. Horns within; they stand.

ARCITE
Lo, cousin, lo, our folly has undone us.

Look, cousin, look, our stupidity is our
downfall.

PALAMON

Why?

ARCITE
This is the Duke, a-hunting as I told you.
If we be found, we are wretched. O, retire
For honor's sake, and safely presently
Into your bush again, sir. We shall find
Too many hours to die in, gentle cousin.
If you be seen, you perish instantly
For breaking prison, and I, if you reveal me,
For my contempt. Then all the world will scorn us,
And say we had a noble difference,
But base disposers of it.

PALAMON
No, no, cousin,
I will no more be hidden, nor put off
This great adventure to a second trial.
I know your cunning, and I know your cause.
He that faints now, shame take him! Put thyself
Upon thy present guard—

ARCITE
You are not mad?

PALAMON
Or I will make th' advantage of this hour
Mine own; and what to come shall threaten me
I fear less than my fortune. Know, weak cousin,
I love Emilia, and in that I'll bury
Thee and all crosses else.

ARCITE
Then come what can come,
Thou shalt know, Palamon, I dare as well
Die as discourse or sleep. Only this fears me,
The law will have the honor of our ends.
Have at thy life!

PALAMON
Look to thine own well, Arcite.

Why?

*This is the Duke, hunting like I told you.
If we are found, we are ruined. Oh, retreat
for the sake of honour, and go back into
the safety of your bush at once, sir.
There is plenty of time for us to die, gentle
cousin. If you are seen, you will be killed at
once for escaping prison, and I, if you expose
me, will get the same for my disobedience. Then
all the world will mock us, and say we had a
noble disagreement, but dealt with it like
peasants.*

*No, no, cousin,
I won't hide any longer, nor postpone
our great test until another time.
I know what you are up to.
Anyone who pulls out now, may he die of
shame! Get on guard–*

Are you mad?

*Or I will turn these events to my
advantage; and whatever is coming my way
frightens me less than my fate. You should
know, weak cousin,
that I love Emilia, and for that I shall bury
you and anyone else who tries to stop me.*

*Then whatever happens
you shall discover, Palamon, it is as easy for
me to die as to talk or sleep. The only thing that
worries me is that the law will have the honour
of taking our lives. I attack your life!*

Guard your own well, Arcite.

Fight again. Horns.

Enter Theseus, Hippolyta, Emilia, Pirithous, and Train.

THESEUS
What ignorant and mad malicious traitors
Are you, that 'gainst the tenor of my laws
Are making battle, thus like knights appointed,
Without my leave and officers of arms?
By Castor, both shall die.

PALAMON
Hold thy word, Theseus.
We are certainly both traitors, both despisers
Of thee and of thy goodness. I am Palamon,
That cannot love thee, he that broke thy
prison—
Think well what that deserves; and this is
Arcite,
A bolder traitor never trod thy ground,
A falser nev'r seem'd friend. This is the man
Was begg'd and banish'd, this is he contemns
thee
And what thou dar'st do; and in this disguise,
Against thy own edict, follows thy sister,
That fortunate bright star, the fair Emilia,
Whose servant (if there be a right in seeing,
And first bequeathing of the soul to) justly
I am, and which is more, dares think her his.
This treachery, like a most trusty lover,
I call'd him now to answer. If thou be'st,
As thou art spoken, great and virtuous,
The true decider of all injuries,
Say, "Fight again!" and thou shalt see me,
Theseus,
Do such a justice thou thyself wilt envy.
Then take my life, I'll woo thee to't.

PIRITHOUS
O heaven,
What more than man is this!

THESEUS
I have sworn.

ARCITE
We seek not
Thy breath of mercy, Theseus. 'Tis to me
A thing as soon to die as thee to say it,
And no more mov'd. Where this man calls me

---

*What ignorant, mad and evil traitors
are you, fighting with each other against
the laws I have laid down, dressed like knights,
without my permission and without my
officials? By Castor, you shall both die.*

*Save your speeches, Theseus.
We are certainly both traitors, we both hate
you and your goodness. I am Palamon,
and I can't love you, I broke out of your prison—
think what punishment that deserves; and this is
Arcite,
a bolder traitor never walked in your country,
there was never such a false friend. This is the
man
who was disgraced and banished, showing
contempt
for you and everything you do; and in this
disguise, against your own ruling, he's
following your sister, that wonderful bright
star, the fair Emilia, whose servant (if the one
who saw her first and first fell in love with her)
I am by rights, and what's more he thinks that
she is his. Like a loyal lover I have now
challenged him to answer for this treachery. If
you are as great and virtuous as they say,
the proper judge of all wrongs,
say, "Fight again!" And you shall see me,
Theseus,
give out justice that you yourself would envy.
Then take my life, I'll beg you to do it.*

*Oh heaven,
who is this, greater than a man!*

I have sworn you will die.

*We're not looking for
your mercy, Theseus. It means as little
to me to die as it does to you to say it,
it doesn't bother me. This man calls me a*

traitor,
Let me say thus much: if in love be treason
In service of so excellent a beauty,
As I love most, and in that faith will perish,
As I have brought my life here to confirm it,
As I have serv'd her truest, worthiest,
As I dare kill this cousin that denies it,
So let me be most traitor, and ye please me.
For scorning thy edict, Duke, ask that lady
Why she is fair, and why her eyes command me
Stay here to love her; and if she say "traitor,"
I am a villain fit to lie unburied.

PALAMON
Thou shalt have pity of us both, O Theseus,
If unto neither thou show mercy. Stop,
As thou art just, thy noble ear against us;
As thou art valiant, for thy cousin's soul,
Whose twelve strong labors crown his memory,
Let 's die together, at one instant, Duke.
Only a little let him fall before me,
That I may tell my soul he shall not have her.

THESEUS
I grant your wish, for to say true, your cousin
Has ten times more offended, for I gave him
More mercy than you found, sir, your offenses
Being no more than his. None here speak for
'em,
For ere the sun set, both shall sleep forever.

HIPPOLYTA
Alas, the pity! Now or never, sister,
Speak, not to be denied. That face of yours
Will bear the curses else of after-ages
For these lost cousins.

EMILIA
In my face, dear sister,
I find no anger to 'em, nor no ruin:
The misadventure of their own eyes kill 'em;
Yet that I will be woman, and have pity,
My knees shall grow to th' ground but I'll get mercy.
Help me, dear sister, in a deed so virtuous
The powers of all women will be with us.

traitor, let me say this about it: if it's treason to be in love with such a wonderful beauty as the one I love most, and to die for it, as I have risked my life coming here to prove it, as I have served her most loyally and worthily, as I am going to kill this cousin who denies it, so let me be a traitor and do as you please with me. If you want a reason for my disobedience, Duke, ask that lady why she is beautiful, why her eyes order me to stay here and love her; and if she says I'm a traitor, I am a villain who doesn't deserve a decent burial.

You would be showing pity for both of us, O Theseus, if you shown no mercy for either. If you are just then block your noble ears against us; as you are brave, for the memory of your cousin, whose twelve great works are still remembered, let us die together, Duke, instantaneously. Just let him die a little before me, so I can be certain he will not have her.

I grant your wish, because truthfully your cousin has offended ten times more than you, for I gave him more mercy than you had, sir, when your crimes were no worse than his. Nobody speak for them, for before the sun sets they shall both be sleeping eternally.

Alas, how terrible! You must speak out fearlessly, sister, now or never. Otherwise you will be cursed by all those who come after us for letting these cousins die.

*I don't have any anger for them, dear sister, and I don't have any desire for them to die: it's their own wandering eyes which will kill them;
but because I am a woman I will show pity, I will go down on my knees to get mercy. Help me, dear sister, do something so virtuous that the power of all women will assist us.*

Most royal brother—

Most royal brother–

They kneel.

HIPPOLYTA
Sir, by our tie of marriage—

Sir, by the bonds of our marriage–

EMILIA
By your own spotless honor—

Through your own spotless honour–

HIPPOLYTA
By that faith,
That fair hand, and that honest heart you gave
me—

By the faith,
the fair hand, and the honest heart that you
gave me–

EMILIA
By that you would have pity in another,
By your own virtues infinite—

As you would wished to be pitied by another,
by your own intimate virtue–

HIPPOLYTA
By valor,
By all the chaste nights I have ever pleas'd
you—

Through your bravery,
for all the pleasure I have given you in the
night–

THESEUS
These are strange conjurings.

These are strange demands.

PIRITHOUS
Nay then I'll in too.

Well, I'll join in too.

Kneels.

By all our friendship, sir, by all our dangers,
By all you love most—wars, and this sweet
lady—

For our friendship, sir, for all our dangers,
by all you love most–war, and this sweet lady–

EMILIA
By that you would have trembled to deny
A blushing maid—

For something that you would be afraid to deny
a blushing girl–

HIPPOLYTA
By your own eyes, by strength,
In which you swore I went beyond all women,
Almost all men, and yet I yielded, Theseus—

For the sake of your own eyes, and my strength,
which is always greater than that of any
woman, and almost all men, and yet I
surrendered to you, Theseus–

PIRITHOUS
To crown all this, by your most noble soul,

On top of everything, for your most noble soul,

Which cannot want due mercy, I beg first.

which cannot be lacking in mercy, I beg you.

HIPPOLYTA
Next hear my prayers.

And hear my prayers next.

EMILIA
Last let me entreat, sir.

And let me beg you last of all, sir.

PIRITHOUS
For mercy.

For mercy.

HIPPOLYTA
Mercy.

Mercy.

EMILIA
Mercy on these princes.

Have mercy on these princes.

THESEUS
Ye make my faith reel. Say I felt
Compassion to 'em both, how would you place it?

You've put my mind in a whirl. What if I felt sorry for them both, what should I do then?

EMILIA
Upon their lives; but with their banishments.

Save their lives, just exile them.

THESEUS
You are a right woman, sister, you have pity,
But want the understanding where to use it.
If you desire their lives, invent a way
Safer than banishment. Can these two live,
And have the agony of love about 'em,
And not kill one another? Every day
They'ld fight about you; hourly bring your honor
In public question with their swords. Be wise then
And here forget 'em; it concerns your credit
And my oath equally. I have said they die;
Better they fall by th' law than one another.
Bow not my honor.

You are a good woman, sister, you have pity, but you don't know how you should apply it. If you want them to live, think of a way safer than exile. Can these two live, both suffering from the agony of love, and not kill each other? Every day they would fight over you; every hour they would duel for your honour in public. So be sensible and forget about them; it affects your reputation and my oath equally. I have said they will die; it's better for them to be executed by the law than each other.
Don't make me be dishonourable.

EMILIA
O my noble brother,
That oath was rashly made, and in your anger,
Your reason will not hold it. If such vows
Stand for express will, all the world must

O my noble brother, you made that oath in the heat of the moment when you were angry, you won't keep to it when you think of it. If such oaths have to be

perish.
Beside, I have another oath 'gainst yours,
Of more authority, I am sure more love,
Not made in passion neither, but good heed.

THESEUS
What is it, sister?

PIRITHOUS
Urge it home, brave lady.

EMILIA
That you would nev'r deny me any thing
Fit for my modest suit and your free granting.
I tie you to your word now; if ye fall in't,
Think how you maim your honor
(For now I am set a-begging, sir, I am deaf
To all but your compassion), how their lives
Might breed the ruin of my name; opinion,
Shall any thing that loves me perish for me?
That were a cruel wisdom. Do men proin
The straight young boughs that blush with
thousand blossoms,
Because they may be rotten? O Duke Theseus,
The goodly mothers that have groan'd for
these,
And all the longing maids that ever lov'd,
If your vow stand, shall curse me and my
beauty,
And in their funeral songs for these two cousins
Despise my cruelty, and cry woe worth me,
Till I am nothing but the scorn of women.
For heaven's sake save their lives, and banish
'em.

THESEUS
On what conditions?

EMILIA
Swear 'em never more
To make me their contention, or to know me,
To tread upon thy dukedom, and to be,
Where ever they shall travel, ever strangers
To one another.

PALAMON

---

maintained then the whole world would die.
Besides, I have another oath to put against
yours,
which is more powerful, has more love in it,
and was made rationally, not out of passion.

What is it, sister?

Drive it home, good lady.

That you would never deny me anything
within your power that was suitable for my
modest position. I hold you to your word now;
if you don't keep it, think what damage you do
your honour (now I have started begging, Sir, I
can't hear anything but your compassion), how
their deaths would ruin my reputation; what
would people think, if anyone who loved me
should die for it? That would be a cruel
judgement. Do men prune straight young
branches that hold a thousand flowers,
because they might be rotten? Oh Duke
Theseus, if you stick to your word the good
mothers who suffered to give these men birth,
and all the longing girls that ever were in love,
shall curse me and my beauty,
and in their funeral songs for these two cousins
they will hate my cruelty, and call for me to
suffer,
until I am hated by all women.
For the sake of heaven save their lives, and
banish them.

On what conditions?

Make them swear they will never
fight over me again, or try to find me,
or walk in your lands, and that
wherever they go they will never
see each other again.

I'll be cut a-pieces
Before I take this oath. Forget I love her?
O all ye gods, despise me then. Thy banishment
I not mislike, so we may fairly carry
Our swords and cause along; else, never trifle,
But take our lives, Duke. I must love, and will,
And for that love must and dare kill this cousin,
On any piece the earth has.

THESEUS
Will you, Arcite,
Take these conditions?

PALAMON
He's a villain then.

PIRITHOUS
These are men!

ARCITE
No, never. Duke. 'Tis worse to me than begging
To take my life so basely. Though I think
I never shall enjoy her, yet I'll preserve
The honor of affection, and die for her,
Make death a devil.

THESEUS
What may be done? For now I feel compassion.

PIRITHOUS
Let it not fall again, sir.

THESEUS
Say, Emilia,
If one of them were dead, as one must, are you
Content to take th' other to your husband?
They cannot both enjoy you. They are princes
As goodly as your own eyes, and as noble
As ever fame yet spoke of. Look upon 'em
And if you can love, end this difference.
I give consent.—Are you content too, princes?

BOTH. ARCITE AND PALAMON
With all our souls.

I'll be cut to pieces
before I swear this. Forget I love her?
Then all the gods can despise me. I don't object
to being exiled, if we can take our swords
and continue our battle; otherwise, don't mess
about, but take our lives, Duke. I must love, and
I will, and for that love I must and there to kill
this cousin, wherever he is on Earth.

Will you agree to these
conditions, Arcite?

He's a villain if he does.

These are truly men!

No, never, Duke. I would rather be a beggar
the man lives my life so dishonourably. Though
I think
I shall never have her, I'll still uphold
the honour of my love, and die for her,
if death were the devil himself.

What can be done? For now I feel pity.

Hold on to that feeling, sir.

Tell me, Emilia,
if one of them was dead, as one of them must
be, are you happy to take the other one as your
husband? They cannot both enjoy you. They are
princes as handsome as your own eyes, and as
noble as any in legend. Look at them and if
you can love one of them, stop this argument.
I give consent.–Do you agree, princes?

With all our souls.

THESEUS
He that she refuses
Must die then.

> Whoever she turns down
> must die then.

BOTH. ARCITE AND PALAMON
Any death thou canst invent, Duke.

> Any death you name, Duke.

PALAMON
If I fall from that mouth, I fall with favor,
And lovers yet unborn shall bless my ashes.

> If I am condemned by that mouth, I will die
> lucky, and future generations of lovers will
> bless my ashes.

ARCITE
If she refuse me, yet my grave will wed me,
And soldiers sing my epitaph.

> If she turns me down, my grave will be like a
> wedding bed,
> and soldiers will sing my epitaph.

THESEUS
Make choice then.

> Make your choice then.

EMILIA
I cannot, sir, they are both too excellent:
For me, a hair shall never fall of these men.

> I cannot, sir, they are both too wonderful:
> I don't want to see any harm come to either of
> them for my sake.

HIPPOLYTA
What will become of 'em?

> What will become of them?

THESEUS
Thus I ordain it,
And by mine honor, once again it stands,
Or both shall die: you shall both to your
country,
And each within this month, accompanied
With three fair knights, appear again in this
place,
In which I'll plant a pyramid; and whether,
Before us that are here, can force his cousin
By fair and knightly strength to touch the pillar,
He shall enjoy her; the other lose his head,
And all his friends; nor shall he grudge to fall,
Nor think he dies with interest in this lady.
Will this content ye?

> This is what I order,
> and by my honour, this must be obeyed
> or you both shall die: you shall both go to your
> country,
> and within a month each of you, accompanied
> by three good knights, will come back to this
> place,
> where I will place a pyramid; and whoever,
> in our presence, can force his cousin
> in a fair and chivalrous duel to touch the pillar,
> he will have first; the other will lose his head,
> and so will his companions; and he will not
> complain or think that he dies with any rights to
> this lady. Will this satisfy you?

PALAMON
Yes. Here, cousin Arcite,
I am friends again till that hour.

> Yes. Come here, cousin Arcite,
> I am your friend again until that time.

ARCITE

I embrace ye.

I embrace you.

THESEUS
Are you content, sister?

Are you satisfied, sister?

EMILIA
Yes, I must, sir,
Else both miscarry.

Yes, I must be, sir,
otherwise they both will die.

THESEUS
Come shake hands again then,
And take heed, as you are gentlemen, this quarrel
Sleep till the hour prefix'd, and hold your course.

Come and shake hands again then,
and make sure, on your honour as gentlemen,
that this quarrel
is over until the time I said, keep your promise.

PALAMON
We dare not fail thee, Theseus.

We do not fail you, Theseus.

THESEUS
Come, I'll give ye
Now usage like to princes and to friends.
When ye return, who wins I'll settle here;
Who loses, yet I'll weep upon his bier.

Come, now I'll treat you as princes and friends
should be treated. When you come back, I will
give whoever wins a position here; whoever
loses, I will weep at his funeral.

Exeunt.

Athens. A room in the prison.

(Jailer, Two Friends, Wooer, Jailer's Brother, Daughter)

Enter Jailer and his Friend.

JAILER
Hear you no more? Was nothing said of me
Concerning the escape of Palamon?
Good sir, remember.

Did you hear anything else? Wasn't anything
said about me regarding Palamon's escape?
Good sir, try to remember.

FIRST FRIEND OF THE JAILER
Nothing that I heard,
For I came home before the business
Was fully ended. Yet I might perceive,
Ere I departed, a great likelihood
Of both their pardons; for Hippolyta,
And fair-ey'd Emily, upon their knees
Begg'd with such handsome pity, that the Duke
Methought stood staggering whether he should follow

I heard nothing,
though I came home before the business
was wrapped up. But I noticed,
before I left, it seemed very likely
that they would both be pardoned; for
Hippolyta and beautiful Emily were begging for
pity so beautifully upon their knees, that the
Duke seemed to me to be wavering between
keeping

His rash oath, or the sweet compassion
Of those two ladies; and to second them,
That truly noble prince Pirithous,
Half his own heart, set in too, that I hope
All shall be well. Neither heard I one question
Of your name, or his scape.

JAILER
Pray heaven it hold so!

SECOND FRIEND OF THE JAILER
Be of good comfort, man; I bring you news,
Good news.

JAILER
They are welcome.

SECOND FRIEND OF THE JAILER
Palamon has clear'd you,
And got your pardon, and discover'd how
And by whose means he escap'd, which was
your daughter's,
Whose pardon is procur'd too; and the
prisoner—
Not to be held ungrateful to her goodness—
Has given a sum of money to her marriage,
A large one, I'll assure you.

JAILER
Ye are a good man
And ever bring good news.

FIRST FRIEND OF THE JAILER
How was it ended?

SECOND FRIEND OF THE JAILER
Why, as it should be: they that nev'r begg'd
But they prevail'd, had their suits fairly
granted:
The prisoners have their lives.

FIRST FRIEND OF THE JAILER
I knew 'twould be so.

SECOND FRIEND OF THE JAILER

*his hasty oath, or showing pity
to those two ladies; and to back them up,
that truly noble Prince Pirithous
threw in his heartfelt opinions, so I hope
all will be well. I didn't hear anyone mention
you, or his escape.*

May heaven keep it that way!

Enter Second Friend.

*Cheer up, man; I bring you news,
good news.*

That would be welcome.

*Palamon has exonerated you,
and you have been pardoned, he has revealed
how
and with whose help he escaped; it was your
daughter who helped him,
she has been pardoned too; and the prisoner–
not wanting to seem ungrateful for her help–
has given her a sum of money for a dowry,
a large one, I can promise you.*

*You are a good man,
always bringing good news.*

How did it finish?

*Why, as it should: those who've never begged
without success had their pleas granted:
the prisoners keep their lives.*

I knew that would happen.

But there be new conditions, which you'll hear of
At better time.

JAILER
I hope they are good.

SECOND FRIEND OF THE JAILER
They are honorable,
How good they'll prove, I know not.

FIRST FRIEND OF THE JAILER
'Twill be known.

WOOER
Alas, sir, where's your daughter?

JAILER
Why do you ask?

WOOER
O sir, when did you see her?

SECOND FRIEND OF THE JAILER
How he looks!

JAILER
This morning.

WOOER
Was she well? Was she in health?
Sir, when did she sleep?

FIRST FRIEND OF THE JAILER
These are strange questions.

JAILER
I do not think she was very well, for, now
You make me mind her, but this very day
I ask'd her questions, and she answered me
So far from what she was, so childishly,
So sillily, as if she were a fool,
An innocent, and I was very angry.
But what of her, sir?

But there are new conditions, which you'll hear of nearer the time.

I hope they are good.

They are honourable,
how good they'll prove to be, I don't know.

We shall see.

Enter Wooer.

Alas, sir, where is your daughter?

Why do you ask?

Oh sir, when did you last see her?

What does he look like!

This morning.

What she well? Was she healthy?
Sir, had she slept?

These are strange questions.

I don't think she is very well, for, now
you make me think of her, just today
I asked her questions, and she answered me
so differently from normal, so childishly,
so stupidly, as if she were a fool,
a baby, and I was very angry.
But what about her, sir?

WOOER
Nothing but my pity.
But you must know it, and as good by me
As by another that less loves her.

JAILER
Well, sir?

FIRST FRIEND OF THE JAILER
Not right?

SECOND FRIEND OF THE JAILER
Not well?

WOOER
No, sir, not well:
'Tis too true, she is mad.

FIRST FRIEND OF THE JAILER
It cannot be.

WOOER
Believe. You'll find it so.

JAILER
I half suspected
What you told me. The gods comfort her!
Either this was her love to Palamon,
Or fear of my miscarrying on his scape,
Or both.

WOOER
'Tis likely.

JAILER
But why all this haste, sir?

WOOER
I'll tell you quickly. As I late was angling
In the great lake that lies behind the palace,
From the far shore, thick set with reeds and sedges,
As patiently I was attending sport,
I heard a voice, a shrill one; and attentive
I gave my ear, when I might well perceive
'Twas one that sung, and by the smallness of it,

Nothing except for my pity.
But you must know about it, and it's just as well
coming from me
as from someone else who loves her less.

Well, sir?

Is she not right?

Not well?

No, sir, not well:
sorry to say, she is mad.

She can't be.

Believe it, you will find she is.

I half suspected
what you told me. May the good gods bring her
comfort! This was caused by her love for
Palamon, or the thought of my being punished
for his escape, or both.

That seems likely.

But why are you in such a hurry, sir?

I'll tell you quickly. As I was fishing recently
in the great lake that lies behind the palace,
I was patiently waiting for a catch
on the far shore, which is thickly covered with
reeds and grass,
I heard a voice, a shrill one; and I listened
carefully, and I realised that it was obviously,
from the littleness of it, sung by

A boy or woman. I then left my angle
To his own skill, came near, but yet perceiv'd
not
Who made the sound, the rushes and the reeds
Had so encompass'd it. I laid me down
And list'ned to the words she sung, for then
Through a small glade cut by the fishermen,
I saw it was your daughter.

JAILER
Pray go on, sir.

WOOER
She sung much, but no sense; only I heard her
Repeat this often, "Palamon is gone,
Is gone to th' wood to gather mulberries.
I'll find him out tomorrow."

FIRST FRIEND OF THE JAILER
Pretty soul!

WOOER
"His shackles will betray him, he'll be taken,
And what shall I do then? I'll bring a bevy,
A hundred black-ey'd maids that love as I do,
With chaplets on their heads of daffadillies,
With cherry lips and cheeks of damask roses,
And all we'll dance an antic 'fore the Duke,
And beg his pardon." Then she talk'd of you,
sir:
That you must lose your head tomorrow
morning,
And she must gather flowers to bury you,
And see the house made handsome. Then she
sung
Nothing but "Willow, willow, willow," and
between
Ever was "Palamon, fair Palamon,"
And "Palamon was a tall young man." The
place
Was knee-deep where she sat; her careless
tresses
A wreath of bulrush rounded; about her stuck
Thousand fresh water-flowers of several colors,
That methought she appear'd like the fair
nymph

a boy or a woman. So I left my hook
to its own devices and went closer, but I
couldn't see who was making the noise, the
rushes and the reeds
were so thick around. I laid down
and listen to the words she was singing, for
then I saw it was your daughter through a small
clearing cut by the fishermen.

Please go on, sir.

She sang a lot, but made no sense; but I heard
her repeat this often; "Palamon is gone,
he's gone into the woods to gather mulberries.
I'll find him tomorrow."

Sweet soul!

"His shackles will give him away, he'll be
captured, and what shall I do then? I'll bring a
group of a hundred black eyed girls that love as
I do, with crowns of daffodils on their heads,
with cherry lips and cheeks blushing pink,
and we'll all dance a mad dance before the
Duke, and beg for his pardon." Then she spoke
of you, sir:
that you would lose your head tomorrow
morning,
and that she must gather flowers for your
funeral, and see that the house was tidy. Then
she sang
nothing but "Willow, Willow, Willow," and in
between
it was always "Palamon, fair Palamon,"
and "Palamon was a tall young man." The
place
she was sitting was knee deep; her careless
hair
was trailing in the bulrushes; all around her
there were a thousand fresh water flowers of
different colours, so I thought that she looked
like the beautiful nymph

That feeds the lake with waters, or as Iris
Newly dropp'd down from heaven. Rings she made
Of rushes that grew by, and to 'em spoke
The prettiest posies—"Thus our true love's tied,"
"This you may loose, not me," and many a one;
And then she wept, and sung again, and sigh'd,
And with the same breath smil'd, and kiss'd her hand.

SECOND FRIEND OF THE JAILER
Alas, what pity it is!

WOOER
I made in to her.
She saw me, and straight sought the flood. I sav'd her,
And set her safe to land; when presently
She slipp'd away, and to the city made
With such a cry and swiftness that, believe me,
She left me far behind her. Three or four
I saw from far off cross her—one of 'em
I knew to be your brother; where she stay'd,
And fell, scarce to be got away. I left them with her,
And hither came to tell you.

Here they are.

JAILER'S DAUGHTER
"May you never more enjoy the light," etc.
Is not this a fine song?

JAILER BROTHER
O, a very fine one!

JAILER'S DAUGHTER
I can sing twenty more.

JAILER BROTHER
I think you can.

JAILER'S DAUGHTER

that runs the waters into the lake, or like Iris
just come down from heaven. She made circlets
out of the nearby rushes, and said the
sweetest little poems to them–"This is how our
true love is tied,"
"you can unite this, not me," and many others;
and then she wept, and sang again, and sighed,
and at the same time smiled, and kissed her
hand.

Alas, what a shame it is!

I went in after her.
She saw me, and tried at once to get to the deep
parts. I saved her,
and got her safely on land; then shortly
she slipped away, and made off for the city
with such noise and speed that, believe me,
she left me far behind. I saw three or four
people accost her from a distance–one of them
I knew was your brother; she stayed with him,
she fell down, they could hardly carry her
away. I left them with her,
and came here to tell you.

Enter Jailer's Brother, Daughter, and others.

Here they are.

Sings.
"May you never enjoy the light again,"
isn't that a fine song?

Oh, a very fine one!

I can sing twenty more.

I think you can.

Yes, truly, can I. I can sing "The Broom,"
And "Bonny Robin." Are not you a tailor?

JAILER BROTHER
Yes.

JAILER'S DAUGHTER
Where's my wedding gown?

JAILER BROTHER
I'll bring it tomorrow.

JAILER'S DAUGHTER
Do, very early, I must be abroad else,
To call the maids and pay the minstrels,
For I must lose my maidenhead by cocklight,
'Twill never thrive else.

"O fair, O sweet," etc.

JAILER BROTHER
You must ev'n take it patiently.

JAILER
'Tis true.

JAILER'S DAUGHTER
Good ev'n, good men. Pray did you ever hear
Of one young Palamon?

JAILER
Yes, wench, we know him.

JAILER'S DAUGHTER
Is't not a fine young gentleman?

JAILER
'Tis, love.

JAILER BROTHER
By no mean cross her, she is then distemper'd
Far worse than now she shows.

FIRST FRIEND OF THE JAILER

---

*Yes, certainly I can. I can sing, "The Broom,"
and "Bonny Robin." Aren't you a tailor?*

I am.

Where's my wedding gown?

I'll bring it tomorrow.

*Do, very early, I have to go out
to summon the bridesmaids and pay the
musicians,
for I must lose my virginity before dawn,
nothing else will do.*

*Sings.
"Oh fair, oh sweet,"*

You must suffer this patiently.

That's true.

*Good evening, good man. Tell me, did you ever
hear of one young Palamon?*

Yes, girl, we know him.

Isn't he a fine young gentleman?

He is, love.

*On no account disagree with her, or she'll be
much madder than she looks now.*

Yes, he's a fine man.

JAILER'S DAUGHTER
O, is he so? You have a sister?

FIRST FRIEND OF THE JAILER
Yes.

JAILER'S DAUGHTER
But she shall never have him, tell her so,
For a trick that I know. Y' had best look to her,
For if she see him once, she's gone—she's done,
And undone in an hour. All the young maids
Of our town are in love with him, but I laugh at 'em
And let 'em all alone. Is't not a wise course?

FIRST FRIEND OF THE JAILER
Yes.

JAILER'S DAUGHTER
There is at least two hundred now with child by him—
There must be four. Yet I keep close for all this,
Close as a cockle. And all these must be boys,
He has the trick on't; and at ten years old
They must be all gelt for musicians,
And sing the wars of Theseus.

SECOND FRIEND OF THE JAILER
This is strange.

JAILER'S DAUGHTER
As ever you heard, but say nothing.

FIRST FRIEND OF THE JAILER
No.

JAILER'S DAUGHTER
They come from all parts of the dukedom to him.
I'll warrant ye he had not so few last night
As twenty to dispatch. He'll tickle't up
In two hours, if his hand be in.

Yes, he's a fine man.

Is he indeed? Have you a sister?

Yes.

But she will never have him, tell her so,
I have the skills. You'd best watch out for her,
for if she sees him one time, she's lost–she's lost,
an done within an hour. All young maids
in our town are in love with him, but I laugh at them
and don't let that bother me. Isn't that sensible?

Yes.

There are at least two hundred now who are pregnant by him—
there must be four. But despite that I keep it secret, closed up like a clam. And they must all be boys,
he knows how to do it; and at ten years old they must all be castrated to make musicians who will sing about the wars of Theseus.

This is strange.

The strangest thing you ever heard, but don't say anything.

No.

They'll come from all over the country to him.
I promise you he didn't have fewer than twenty to deal with last night. He'll do the business
in two hours, if he's in good form.

JAILER
She's lost
Past all cure.

She's gone
past curing.

JAILER BROTHER
Heaven forbid, man!

Heaven forbid, man!

JAILER'S DAUGHTER
Come hither, you are a wise man.

To the Jailer.
Come here, you are wise man.

FIRST FRIEND OF THE JAILER
Does she know him?

Does she recognise him?

SECOND FRIEND OF THE JAILER
No, would she did!

No, I wish she did!

JAILER'S DAUGHTER
You are master of a ship?

Are you the captain of a ship?

JAILER
Yes.

Yes.

JAILER'S DAUGHTER
Where's your compass?

Where's your compass?

JAILER
Here.

Here.

JAILER'S DAUGHTER
Set it to th' north.
And now direct your course to th' wood, where Palamon
Lies longing for me. For the tackling
Let me alone. Come weigh, my hearts, cheerly!

Point it North.
And now set your course for the wood, where Palamon
is lying waiting for me. For dealing with the tackle, you can leave that to me. Pull away, brave lads, pull away!

ALL.
Owgh, owgh, owgh!

Oh, oh, oh!

JAILER'S DAUGHTER
'Tis up! The wind's fair.
Top the bowling! Out with the mainsail!
Where's your whistle, master?

The sail's up! The wind's in our favour.
Tie up the bowline! Out with the mainsail!
Where's your whistle, master?

JAILER BROTHER
Let's get her in.

Let's get her indoors.

JAILER
Up to the top, boy!

Up to the crowsnest, boy!

JAILER BROTHER
Where's the pilot?

Where's the pilot?

FIRST FRIEND OF THE JAILER
Here.

Here.

JAILER'S DAUGHTER
What ken'st thou?

What can you see?

SECOND FRIEND OF THE JAILER
A fair wood.

A beautiful wood.

JAILER'S DAUGHTER
Bear for it, master.
Tack about!
Sings.
"When Cynthia with her borrowed light," etc.

Head for it, master.
Swing around!
[Sings]
"When Cynthia with her borrowed light [etc]"

Exeunt.

A room in the palace.

(Emilia, Gentleman, Theseus, Hippolyta, Pirithous, Attendants, Messenger)

Enter Emilia alone, with two pictures.

EMILIA
Yet I may bind those wounds up, that must open
And bleed to death for my sake else. I'll choose,
And end their strife. Two such young handsome men
Shall never fall for me; their weeping mothers,
Following the dead-cold ashes of their sons,
Shall never curse my cruelty. Good heaven,
What a sweet face has Arcite! If wise Nature,
With all her best endowments, all those beauties
She sows into the births of noble bodies,
Were here a mortal woman, and had in her
The coy denials of young maids, yet doubtless
She would run mad for this man. What an eye,
Of what a fiery sparkle and quick sweetness,
Has this young prince! Here Love himself sits

But maybe I can bandage these wounds, that must open
and cause fatal bleeding for me otherwise. I'll choose one
and end their fight. I won't let two such handsome
young men die for me; their weeping mothers
will never curse my cruelty as they follow the
cold dead ashes of their sons. Good heavens,
what a sweet face Arcite has! If wise Nature,
with all her best qualities, all those accomplishments
she implants in noble people at birth,
was a mortal woman, and kept to
the coy rebuttals of young virgins, she would
still lose her head over this man. What
a sweet and sparkling fiery look this young
prince has in his eyes! He looks like love itself.

smiling.
Just such another wanton Ganymede
Set Jove afire with, and enforc'd the god
Snatch up the goodly boy and set him by him,
A shining constellation. What a brow,
Of what a spacious majesty, he carries,
Arch'd like the great-ey'd Juno's, but far
sweeter,
Smoother than Pelops' shoulder! Fame and
Honor
Methinks from hence, as from a promontory
Pointed in heaven, should clap their wings and
sing
To all the under world the loves and fights
Of gods and such men near 'em. Palamon
Is but his foil, to him, a mere dull shadow;
He's swarth and meagre, of an eye as heavy
As if he had lost his mother; a still temper,
No stirring in him, no alacrity,
Of all this sprightly sharpness, not a smile.
Yet these that we count errors may become
him:
Narcissus was a sad boy, but a heavenly.
O, who can find the bent of woman's fancy?
I am a fool, my reason is lost in me;
I have no choice, and I have lied so lewdly
That women ought to beat me. On my knees
I ask thy pardon: Palamon, thou art alone
And only beautiful, and these the eyes,
These the bright lamps of beauty, that
command
And threaten Love, and what young maid dare
cross 'em?
What a bold gravity, and yet inviting,
Has this brown manly face! O Love, this only
From this hour is complexion. Lie there, Arcite,
Thou art a changeling to him, a mere gypsy,
And this the noble body. I am sotted,
Utterly lost. My virgin's faith has fled me;
For if my brother but even now had ask'd me
Whether I lov'd, I had run mad for Arcite;
Now if my sister—more for Palamon.
Stand both together: now, come ask me,
brother—
Alas, I know not! Ask me now, sweet sister—
I may go look! What a mere child is fancy,

He looks just like Ganymede, who
inflamed Jove and made him kidnap
the handsome boy and place him at his side
in a shining constellation. What a forehead,
how majestically broad, he has,
curved like great-eyed Juno's, but far sweeter,
smoother than Pelop's shoulder! I think
Fame and Honour should sit there as if
it were a clifftop in heaven, and clap their
wings
and sing to everyone below about the loves and
fights
of gods and men who are almost gods.
Palamon
is just a pale copy of him, a dull shadow;
he's dark and feeble, with such a gloomy
expression
you'd think his mother had just died; he's quiet,
there's no life or vigour to him, he doesn't show
any sort of spirit, not even a smile.
But what I call deficiencies might suit him;
Narcissus was a gloomy lad, but divine.
Oh, who knows what attracts a woman?
I am a fool, I've lost my mind;
I have no choice, and I've lied so lustfully
that women ought to beat me. I beg for your
pardon on my knees: Palamon, you are unique
and the only
beautiful one, and these are the eyes,
the bright lamps of beauty, that offer and
demand love, and what young girl can resist?
What strong seriousness, but still attractive,
this brown manly face has! Oh love, from now
on this is the only colour for me. Stay there,
Arcite,
you are a substitute for him, just a gypsy boy,
and this is the true nobleman. I am besotted,
utterly lost. My maidenly confidence has
deserted me;
if my brother had asked me just now
if I was in love, I would have been dizzy for
Arcite; if my sister asked, I would have been for
Palamon.
Put them both together; now, ask me brother -
alas, I don't know! Ask me now, sweet sister-
I'll have to look! Attraction is like a child,

That having two fair gauds of equal sweetness,
Cannot distinguish, but must cry for both!

that won't choose between two toys of equal value, but cries to have them both!

Enter Gentleman.

How now, sir?

What is it, sir?

GENTLEMAN
From the noble Duke your brother,
Madam, I bring you news. The knights are
come.

I bring you news, madam, from your brother, the noble Duke. The knights have come.

EMILIA
To end the quarrel?

To end their argument?

GENTLEMAN
Yes.

Yes.

EMILIA
Would I might end first!
What sins have I committed, chaste Diana,
That my unspotted youth must now be soil'd
With blood of princes? And my chastity
Be made the altar where the lives of lovers—
Two greater and two better never yet
Made mothers joy—must be the sacrifice
To my unhappy beauty?

I wish I could die first! What sins have I committed, pure Diana, that my blameless youth must be stained with the blood of princes? And my chastity turned into an altar where the lives of two lovers- the greatest and best ones that ever gave their mothers joy- must be sacrificed to my unhappy beauty?

Enter Theseus, Hippolyta, Pirithous, and Attendants.

THESEUS
Bring 'em in
Quickly, by any means, I long to see 'em.—
Your two contending lovers are return'd,
And with them their fair knights. Now, my fair
sister,
You must love one of them.

Bring them in as quickly as you like, I'm longing to see them. Your two competing lovers have returned, bringing their fair knights with them. Now, my fair sister, you must choose one of them.

EMILIA
I had rather both,
So neither for my sake should fall untimely.

I would rather have both, so that neither would die an early death for me.

THESEUS
Who saw 'em?

Who saw them?

PIRITHOUS
I a while.

I did, a while ago.

GENTLEMAN
And I.

THESEUS
From whence come you, sir?

1. MESSENGER
From the knights.

THESEUS
Pray speak,
You that have seen them, what they are.

1. MESSENGER
I will, sir,
And truly what I think. Six braver spirits
Than these they have brought (if we judge by
the outside)
I never saw nor read of. He that stands
In the first place with Arcite, by his seeming
Should be a stout man, by his face a prince
(His very looks so say him), his complexion
Nearer a brown than black; stern, and yet noble,
Which shows him hardy, fearless, proud of
dangers.
The circles of his eyes show fire within him,
And as a heated lion, so he looks;
His hair hangs long behind him, black and
shining
Like ravens' wings; his shoulders broad and
strong,
Arm'd long and round, and on his thigh a
sword
Hung by a curious baldrick, when he frowns
To seal his will with. Better, o' my conscience,
Was never soldier's friend.

THESEUS
Thou hast well describ'd him.

PIRITHOUS
Yet a great deal short,
Methinks, of him that's first with Palamon.

THESEUS

And I.

Enter First Messenger.

Where have you come from, sir?

From the knights.

*You've seen them,
please tell us who they are.*

*I will, sir,
and give you my honest opinion. I have never
heard of or read about six better men than the
ones they have
brought, if we judge by appearances. He that
stands next to Arcite looks like a very sound
man, his looks show him to be a prince, his
complexion is nearer
to brown than black; stern, and yet noble,
he looks strong, fearless, indifferent to danger.
his eyes show he has a fire within him,
he resembles a rampant lion;
his hair hangs down his back, black and
shining
like ravens' wings; his shoulders are broad and
strong,
his arms long and muscular, and at his waist he
has
a sword hung on a strange sash, to reinforce
his
will when he is angry. I swear you could never
see a better friend for a soldier.*

You have described him well.

*But he doesn't match up, I think,
to the one by Palamon's side.*

Pray speak him, friend.

Please tell us about him, friend.

PIRITHOUS

I guess he is a prince too,
And if it may be, greater; for his show
Has all the ornament of honor in't.
He's somewhat bigger than the knight he spoke of,
But of a face far sweeter; his complexion
Is, as a ripe grape, ruddy. He has felt
Without doubt what he fights for, and so apter
To make this cause his own. In 's face appears
All the fair hopes of what he undertakes,
And when he's angry, then a settled valor
(Not tainted with extremes) runs through his body,
And guides his arm to brave things. Fear he cannot,
He shows no such soft temper. His head's yellow,
Hard-hair'd, and curl'd, thick twin'd like ivy-tods,
Not to undo with thunder. In his face
The livery of the warlike maid appears,
Pure red and white, for yet no beard has blest him;
And in his rolling eyes sits victory,
As if she ever meant to crown his valor.
His nose stands high, a character of honor;
His red lips, after fights, are fit for ladies.

*I guess he is a prince as well,
and if possible a greater one; his appearance
has all the signs of greatness.
He's rather bigger than the knight he spoke of,
but with a much sweeter face; his complexion
is as red as a ripe grape. He has obviously
been in love,
and this makes him more likely
to join in this fight. In his face one can see
all the sweet hopes of what he's doing,
and when he's angry, then a calm bravery
(not spoilt with temper) runs through his body
which guides his hand to great deeds. He
knows no fear,
he's a stranger to such weak emotions. His hair
is blond, with thick curly hair like ivy,
that couldn't be parted by thunder. Facially
he looks like a soldierly girl,
pure red and white, for he has no beard;
Victory shows in his roving eye, as if
she meant to reward his bravery.
he has a noble high arched nose;
his red lips would suit the ladies, after battle.*

EMILIA

Must these men die too?

Are these men going to have to die too?

PIRITHOUS

When he speaks, his tongue
Sounds like a trumpet. All his lineaments
Are as a man would wish 'em, strong and clean.
He wears a well-steel'd axe, the staff of gold.
His age some five and twenty.

*When he speaks, his tongue
Rings out like a trumpet. All the lines of his
body are just as a man would wish, strong and
clean. He carries sharp axe with a golden shaft.
He is around twenty five years old.*

1. MESSENGER

There's another,
A little man, but of a tough soul, seeming
As great as any. Fairer promises
In such a body yet I never look'd on.

*There's another,
a little man, but hardy, who seems
as great as any of them. I never saw
anyone who showed such promise.*

PIRITHOUS
O, he that's freckle-fac'd?

Oh, the one with freckles?

1. MESSENGER
The same, my lord.
Are they not sweet ones?

The same one, my lord.
They look good, don't they?

PIRITHOUS
Yes, they are well.

They certainly do.

1. MESSENGER
Methinks,
Being so few and well dispos'd, they show
Great and fine art in nature. He's white-hair'd,
Not wanton white, but such a manly color
Next to an auburn; tough and nimble set,
Which shows an active soul; his arms are brawny,
Lin'd with strong sinews; to the shoulder-piece
Gently they swell, like women new conceiv'd,
Which speaks him prone to labor, never fainting
Under the weight of arms; stout-hearted, still,
But when he stirs, a tiger. He's grey-ey'd,
Which yields compassion where he conquers; sharp
To spy advantages, and where he finds 'em,
He's swift to make 'em his. He does no wrongs,
Nor takes none. He's round-fac'd, and when he smiles
He shows a lover, when he frowns, a soldier.
About his head he wears the winner's oak,
And in it stuck the favor of his lady.
His age some six and thirty. In his hand
He bears a charging-staff emboss'd with silver.

I think,
with so few of them so well placed, they show
themselves as great works of nature. He's
white-haired, not the white of excess, but such a
manly colour it's as good as auburn; he's tough
and agile, which shows an active soul; his arms
are strong,
lined with big muscles; they gently swell up
to his shoulder, like a just pregnant woman,
which show he is made for work, he never
faints
under the weight of his weapons; he's
stouthearted, calm, but when he gets going he's
a tiger. He has grey eyes
which show pity on those over whom he
triumphs; they are quick to spot advantages,
and when he sees them, he quickly takes hold of
them. He does no wrong and allows nobody to
do him wrong. He has a round face,
and when he smiles he looks like a lover, when
he frowns, a soldier. He wears the victor's
laurel wreath round his head, with a sign of his
lady stuck in it. He is thirty six. In his hand
he carries a fighting stick covered with silver.

THESEUS
Are they all thus?

Are they all like this?

PIRITHOUS
They are all the sons of honor.

They are all the sons of honour.

THESEUS
Now as I have a soul I long to see 'em.
Lady, you shall see men fight now.

Now I swear I'm longing to see them.
Lady, you will see men fight now.

HIPPOLYTA
I wish it,
But not the cause, my lord. They would show
Bravely about the titles of two kingdoms.
'Tis pity love should be so tyrannous.
O my soft-hearted sister, what think you?
Weep not, till they weep blood. Wench, it must
be.

I like that,
but not the reason, my lord. They would
embellish the royalty of two kingdoms.
It's a pity love should be such a tyrant.
Oh, my softhearted sister, what do you think?
Don't weep, until they weep blood. Girl, it's got
to happen.

THESEUS
You have steel'd 'em with your beauty.—
Honor'd friend,
To you I give the field; pray order it,
Fitting the persons that must use it.

Your beauty has armed them.—Honoured friend,
I hand the battlefield to you; please arrange it
so it's suitable for the people who will be using
it.

PIRITHOUS
Yes, sir.

Yes, sir.

THESEUS
Come, I'll go visit 'em. I cannot stay—
Their fame has fir'd me so—till they appear.
Good friend, be royal.

Come on, I'll go and visit them. I can't wait—
the report of them sounds so good—until they
appear. Good friend, act like a king.

PIRITHOUS
There shall want no bravery.

There'll be no good thing missing.

EMILIA
Poor wench, go weep, for whosoever wins
Loses a noble cousin for thy sins.

Poor girl, go and weep, for whoever wins
will lose a noble cousin on account of you.

Exeunt.

A room in the prison.

(Jailer, Wooer, Doctor, Daughter)

Enter Jailer, Wooer, Doctor.

DOCTOR
Her distraction is more at some time of the
moon than at other some, is it not?

Her madness is worse at some phases of the
moon than at others, isn't it?

JAILER
She is continually in a harmless distemper,
sleeps little, altogether without appetite, save
often drinking, dreaming of another world and
a better; and what broken piece of matter soe'er
she's about, the name Palamon lards it, that she
farces ev'ry business withal, fits it to every

She is continually harmlessly deranged, she
sleeps little, she has no appetite, except she
drinks a lot, dreaming of another world, a
better one; whatever broken speech she utters,
it's always full of the name Palamon, she
includes him everything she talks about.

question.

Look where she comes, you shall perceive her behavior.

Enter Daughter.

Here she comes, you will see what she's like.

JAILER'S DAUGHTER
I have forgot it quite; the burden on't was "Down-a, down-a," and penn'd by no worse man than Giraldo, Emilia's schoolmaster. He's as fantastical, too, as ever he may go upon 's legs, for in the next world will Dido see Palamon, and then will she be out of love with Aeneas.

I've completely forgotten it; the chorus of it was "down–a, down–a," written by as good a man as Giraldo, Amelia's schoolmaster. He's got as good an imagination as any man alive, for in the next world Dido will see Palamon, and she won't love Aeneas any more.

DOCTOR
What stuff's here? Poor soul!

What's all this? Poor soul!

JAILER
Ev'n thus all day long.

She's like this all day long.

JAILER'S DAUGHTER
Now for this charm that I told you of, you must bring a piece of silver on the tip of your tongue, or no ferry. Then, if it be your chance to come where the blessed spirits—as there's a sight now! We maids that have our livers perish'd, crack'd to pieces with love, we shall come there, and do nothing all day long but pick flowers with Proserpine. Then will I make Palamon a nosegay, then let him mark me— then—

Now as for this charm I told you about, you must bring a silver coin on the tip of your tongue, or you can't get the ferry. Then, if you happen to come where the blessed spirits are— What a sight that is! We maids whose livers have perished, cracked to pieces with love, we shall go there, and do nothing all day long but pick flowers with Prosperine. Then I will make Palamon a bouquet, then let him notice me— then—

DOCTOR
How prettily she's amiss! Note her a little further.

How sweetly she's gone astray! Let's watch her a little more.

JAILER'S DAUGHTER
Faith, I'll tell you; sometime we go to barley-break, we of the blessed. Alas, 'tis a sore life they have i' th' tother place, such burning, frying, boiling, hissing, howling, chatt'ring, cursing! O, they have shrowd measure! Take heed: if one be mad, or hang or drown themselves, thither they go—Jupiter bless us!— and there shall we be put in a cauldron of lead

I swear, I'll tell you; sometimes we blessed ones play hide and seek. Alas, they have a terrible life in the other place, there's such burning, frying, boiling, hissing, howling, chattering, cursing! Oh, they have a hard punishment! Be warned: if someone is mad, or hangs or drowns themselves, that's where they go–Jupiter bless us!–And we will be put in a cauldron of lead and usurers' grease, amongst a whole million of cutpurses, and there boil like a gammon of bacon that will never be enough.

DOCTOR
How her brain coins!

JAILER'S DAUGHTER
Lords and courtiers that have got maids with child, they are in this place. They shall stand in fire up to the nav'l, and in ice up to th' heart, and there th' offending part burns, and the deceiving part freezes: in troth a very grievous punishment, as one would think, for such a trifle. Believe me, one would marry a leprous witch to be rid on't, I'll assure you.

DOCTOR
How she continues this fancy! 'Tis not an engraff'd madness, but a most thick and profound melancholy.

JAILER'S DAUGHTER
To hear there a proud lady and a proud city-wife howl together! I were a beast and I'ld call it good sport. One cries, "O, this smoke!" th' other, "This fire!" One cries, "O, that ever I did it behind the arras!" and then howls; th' other curses a suing fellow and her garden-house.

Sings.
"I will be true, my stars, my fate," etc.

JAILER
What think you of her, sir?

DOCTOR
I think she has a perturb'd mind, which I cannot minister to.

JAILER
Alas, what then?

and moneylenders' grease, amongst a million thieves, and there we will boil like gammon for ever.

Exit.

How she creates fantasies!

Enter Daughter.

Lords and courtiers who have got girls pregnant, this is where they are. They will stand in fire up to the navel, and in ice up to the heart, so that the part of their body that did wrong burns, and the part that deceived freezes: really a very harsh punishment, one would think, for such a little thing. Believe me, one would marry a leprous witch to escape it.

How she persists with this fantasy! This isn't an ingrained madness, but a deep and profound depression.

To hear a proud lady and a proud bourgeois wailing together! You'd be dumb not find it entertaining. One cries, "Oh, this smoke!" The other one, "This fire!" One cries, "Oh, I wish I had never done it behind the curtain!" And then wails; the other curses the fellow who kept asking her, whom she met in her garden house. [Sings]
"I will be true, my stars, my fate," etc

Exit Daughter.

What you think of her, sir?

I think she has a disturbed mind, which I can't treat.

Alas, then what can we do?

DOCTOR

Understand you she ever affected any man ere she beheld Palamon?

Do you know if she ever fancied any man before she saw Palamon?

JAILER

I was once, sir, in great hope she had fix'd her liking on this gentleman, my friend.

Once upon a time, sir, I was very hopeful that she would choose this gentleman, my friend.

WOOER

I did think so too, and would account I had a great penn'worth on't to give half my state that both she and I at this present stood unfeignedly on the same terms.

I hoped so too, and I would think it was a good bargain to give half of my wealth for us to be honestly on the same terms.

DOCTOR

That intemp'rate surfeit of her eye hath distemper'd the other senses. They may return and settle again to execute their preordain'd faculties, but they are now in a most extravagant vagary. This you must do: confine her to a place where the light may rather seem to steal in than be permitted. Take upon you, young sir her friend, the name of Palamon, say you come to eat with her, and to commune of love. This will catch her attention, for this her mind beats upon; other objects that are inserted 'tween her mind and eye become the pranks and friskins of her madness. Sing to her such green songs of love as she says Palamon hath sung in prison. Come to her, stuck in as sweet flowers as the season is mistress of, and thereto make an addition of some other compounded odors which are grateful to the sense. All this shall become Palamon, for Palamon can sing, and Palamon is sweet, and ev'ry good thing. Desire to eat with her, carve her, drink to her, and still among intermingle your petition of grace and acceptance into her favor. Learn what maids have been her companions and play-feres, and let them repair to her with Palamon in their mouths, and appear with tokens, as if they suggested for him. It is a falsehood she is in, which is with falsehoods to be combated. This may bring her to eat, to sleep, and reduce what's now out of square in her into their former law and regiment. I have seen it

The dizzy excesses of what she has seen has disturbed her other senses. They may return again to perform their natural functions, but for the moment they are wandering everywhere. This is what you must do: shut her up in a place where she is sealed off from daylight. You, young Sir, her friend, pretend you are Palamon, say you've come to eat with her, and to talk of love. This will capture her attention, for this is what she is obsessed with; other things that she sees just become the playthings of her madness. Sing her such youthful songs of love like the ones she says Palamon sang in prison. Come to her carrying whatever sweet flowers this season provides, and so create an atmosphere of sweetness. All this will make her think you are Palamon, for Palamon can sing, and Palamon is sweet, and everything else good. Ask to eat with her, serve her, drink toasts to her, and amongst everything else mix in your requests for her to accept you. Find out what girls have been her companions and playmates, and let them visit her talking about Palamon, bringing presents as if they came from him. She is living a lie, and it must be fought with lies. This may cause her to eat, to sleep, and to regain her senses. I have seen this happen so many times I can't count them, and I have great hopes that this will make the number greater. In between the acts of this project I will come in with my cures. Let us try this plan;

approv'd, how many times I know not, but to make the number more I have great hope in this. I will, between the passages of this project, come in with my appliance. Let us put it in execution; and hasten the success, which doubt not will bring forth comfort.

the quicker the better, and have no doubt that it will work.

Exeunt.

Act IV

Scene I

Before the Temples of Mars, Venus, and Diana.

(Theseus, Pirithous, Hippolyta, Attendants, Palamon, Arcite, Knights, Emilia)

Three altars erected—to Mars, Venus, and Diana. Flourish. Enter Theseus, Pirithous, Hippolyta, Attendants.

THESEUS
Now let 'em enter, and before the gods
Tender their holy prayers. Let the temples
Burn bright with sacred fires, and the altars
In hallowed clouds commend their swelling
incense
To those above us. Let no due be wanting;
They have a noble work in hand will honor
The very powers that love 'em.

Now let them come in, and offer their holy prayers to the gods. Let the temples burn bright with sacred fires, and let the altars offer their billowing clouds of sacred incense to those above us. Make sure all proper ceremony is done; they are performing a noble task which will honour the gods who love them.

Flourish of cornets. Enter Palamon and Arcite and their Knights

PIRITHOUS
Sir, they enter.

Sir, here they come.

THESEUS
You valiant and strong-hearted enemies,
You royal germane foes, that this day come
To blow that nearness out that flames between
ye,
Lay by your anger for an hour, and dove-like,
Before the holy altars of your helpers,
The all-fear'd gods, bow down your stubborn
bodies.
Your ire is more than mortal; so your help be;
And as the gods regard ye, fight with justice.
I'll leave you to your prayers, and betwixt ye
I part my wishes.

You brave and strong hearted enemies, you royal related foes, this day has come which destroys the closeness between you, but put aside your anger for an hour, and peacefully, in front of the holy altars of your helpers, the gods that all fear, bow down your stubborn bodies. Your anger is more than mortal, so your help will be the same; fight fairly, as the gods are watching you. I'll leave you to your prayers, and you both have my good wishes equally.

PIRITHOUS
Honor crown the worthiest!

May the best man win!

Exeunt Theseus and his Train.

PALAMON
The glass is running now that cannot finish

The clock is now ticking and it cannot stop

Till one of us expire. Think you but thus,
That were there aught in me which strove to
show
Mine enemy in this business, were't one eye
Against another, arm oppress'd by arm,
I would destroy th' offender, coz, I would,
Though parcel of myself. Then from this gather
How I should tender you.

ARCITE
I am in labor
To push your name, your ancient love, our
kindred,
Out of my memory; and i' th' self-same place
To seat something I would confound. So hoist
we
The sails that must these vessels port even
where
The heavenly limiter pleases.

PALAMON
You speak well.
Before I turn, let me embrace thee, cousin.

This I shall never do again.

ARCITE
One farewell.

PALAMON
Why, let it be so; farewell, coz.

ARCITE
Farewell, sir.

Knights, kinsmen, lovers, yea, my sacrifices,
True worshippers of Mars, whose spirit in you
Expels the seeds of fear, and th' apprehension
Which still is farther off it, go with me
Before the god of our profession. There
Require of him the hearts of lions and
The breath of tigers, yea, the fierceness too,

---

until one of us is dead. Please note this,
that if anything within me tried to
fight against me in this business, if my eyes
fought each other, my arms wrestled each
other,
I would destroy that thing, cousin, I would,
even though it was part of myself. So you must
see how I must treat you.

I'm doing my best
to forget your name, our long-lasting love, and
relationship;
in the same place I'm going to make you
something
I will destroy. So we begin our journey
and leave it to the gods to see where it ends.

Well said.
Before I turn away, let me embrace you, cousin.

They embrace.

I shall never do this again.

Let's wish each other farewell.

Let it be; farewell, cousin.

Farewell, sir.

Exeunt Palamon and his Knights.

Knights, kinsmen, lovers, yes, my sacrifices,
true worshippers of Mars, whose spirit
drives fear out of you, and the dread
which inspires it, come with me
before the god of our profession.
Ask him for the hearts of lions and
the breath of tigers, yes, the fierceness too,

Yea, the speed also—to go on, I mean,
Else wish we to be snails. You know my prize
Must be dragg'd out of blood; force and great feat
Must put my garland on, where she sticks
The queen of flowers. Our intercession then
Must be to him that makes the camp a cestron
Brimm'd with the blood of men. Give me your aid
And bend your spirits towards him.

and the speed–to go forward, I mean,
otherwise ask that we can be snails. You know my prize
can only be won with bloodshed; strength and skill
must bring me the victor's crown of flowers.
So we must pray to the one who makes the battlefield
a tank brimming with men's blood. Help me
by offering your prayers to him.

They advance to the altar of Mars and fall on their faces; then kneel.

Thou mighty one, that with thy power hast turn'd
Green Neptune into purple; whose approach
Comets prewarn, whose havoc in vast field
Unearthed skulls proclaim, whose breath blows down
The teeming Ceres' foison, who dost pluck
With hand armipotent from forth blue clouds
The mason'd turrets, that both mak'st and break'st
The stony girths of cities: me thy pupil,
Youngest follower of thy drum, instruct this day
With military skill, that to thy laud
I may advance my streamer, and by thee
Be styl'd the lord o' th' day. Give me, great Mars,
Some token of thy pleasure.

*You mighty one, whose power has turned
the green sea into purple; whose coming
is foretold by comets, whose chaos on the battlefield
is shown by discovered skulls, whose breath blows down
the growing crops, who reaches out with his
powerful armoured hand from the blue clouds
and pulls down the brick castles, makes and breaks
the stone walls of cities: teach me today, your pupil,
the youngest of your followers, to have
military skill, so that I can praise you
by raising my flag when I am crowned
victorious by you. Give me, great Mars,
some sign of your approval.*

Here they fall on their faces as formerly, and there is heard clanging of armor, with a short thunder, as the burst of a battle, whereupon they all rise and bow to the altar.

O great corrector of enormous times,
Shaker of o'er-rank states, thou grand decider
Of dusty and old titles, that heal'st with blood
The earth when it is sick, and cur'st the world
O' th' plurisy of people! I do take
Thy signs auspiciously, and in thy name
To my design march boldly.—Let us go.

*Oh great corrector of disordered times,
punisher of corrupt states, you great arbitrator
of ancient titles, who heals the Earth with blood
when it is sick, and rids the world of its
superfluous population! I take your
sign as offering good luck, and I march boldly
to fulfil my plans in your name.–Let us go.*

Exeunt.

Enter Palamon and his Knights, with the former observance.

PALAMON

Our stars must glister with new fire, or be
Today extinct. Our argument is love,
Which if the goddess of it grant, she gives
Victory too. Then blend your spirits with mine,
You whose free nobleness do make my cause
Your personal hazard. To the goddess Venus
Commend we our proceeding, and implore
Her power unto our party.

*Our stars must shine with a new light, or be
put out today. We are fighting for love,
and if the goddess of it gives you that, she gives
you victory too. So join your spirits with mine,
you noblemen who freely choose to risk
yourselves for my sake. We offer our efforts to
the goddess Venus,
and beg her to give strength to our cause.*

Here they advance to the altar of Venus, and fall on their faces; then kneel, as formerly.

Hail, sovereign queen of secrets, who hast power
To call the fiercest tyrant from his rage,
And weep unto a girl; that hast the might,
Even with an eye-glance, to choke Mars's drum
And turn th' alarm to whispers; that canst make
A cripple flourish with his crutch, and cure him
Before Apollo; that mayst force the king
To be his subject's vassal, and induce
Stale gravity to dance; the poll'd bachelor,
Whose youth, like wanton boys through bonfires,
Have skipp'd thy flame, at seventy thou canst catch,
And make him, to the scorn of his hoarse throat,
Abuse young lays of love. What godlike power
Hast thou not power upon? To Phoebus thou
Add'st flames, hotter than his; the heavenly fires
Did scorch his mortal son, thine him. The huntress
All moist and cold, some say, began to throw
Her bow away, and sigh. Take to thy grace
Me thy vow'd soldier, who do bear thy yoke
As 'twere a wreath of roses, yet is heavier
Than lead itself, stings more than nettles. I
Have never been foul-mouth'd against thy law,
Nev'r reveal'd secret, for I knew none—would not,
Had I kenn'd all that were. I never practiced
Upon man's wife, nor would the libels read
Of liberal wits. I never at great feasts
Sought to betray a beauty, but have blush'd

*Hail, Royal Queen of secrets, who has the power
to calm down the fiercest tyrant and make him
weep to a girl; who has the strength to muffle
the drum of Mars with a glance,
and make battle cries into whispers; who can
make a cripple wave his crutch, and cure him
before Apollo can; who can force the King
to serve his subject, and make
serious old men dance; the bald bachelor,
who skipped through your flame in his youth
like a reckless boy leaping a bonfire, you can
catch
him at seventy and make him torture to his sore
throat
singing the love songs of the young. What god
is there whom you cannot master? You add
flames
to the sun, hotter than his; the heavenly fires
burnt his mortal son, yours burned him. Diana,
all moist and cold, some say, gave up in
despair.
Give your Grace to me, your sworn soldier,
who carries your burden as if it were a bunch
of roses, although it is heavier
that led itself, and stings more than nettles. I
have never blasphemed against your law,
never revealed any of your secrets, for I knew
none–
but I would not, if I had known all there were. I
never
cheated with anyone's wife, or would read the
lying gossip of licentious wits. I have never
gone to great feasts and tried to lead a beauty*

At simp'ring sirs that did. I have been harsh
To large confessors, and have hotly ask'd them
If they had mothers; I had one, a woman,
And women 'twere they wrong'd. I knew a man
Of eighty winters—this I told them—who
A lass of fourteen brided. 'Twas thy power
To put life into dust: the aged cramp
Had screw'd his square foot round,
The gout had knit his fingers into knots,
Torturing convulsions from his globy eyes
Had almost drawn their spheres, that what was life
In him seem'd torture. This anatomy
Had by his young fair fere a boy, and I
Believ'd it was his, for she swore it was,
And who would not believe her? Brief, I am
To those that prate and have done, no companion;
To those that boast and have not, a defier;
To those that would and cannot, a rejoicer.
Yea, him I do not love that tells close offices
The foulest way, nor names concealments in
The boldest language. Such a one I am,
And vow that lover never yet made sigh
Truer than I. O then, most soft sweet goddess,
Give me the victory of this question, which
Is true love's merit, and bless me with a sign
Of thy great pleasure.

astray, but have been embarrassed by the simpering men who did. I have been stern to those who bragged, and angrily asked them if they had mothers; I had one, who was a woman, and it was women they were insulting. I knew a man of eighty–this is what I told them–who married a lass of fourteen. It was your power that put life into dust: rheumatism had twisted his feet around, gout had tied his fingers in knots, his bulging eyes had almost been torn from their sockets by painful fits, so that life was a torture to him. This old body had a boy with this young beauty, and I believed it was his, for she swore it was, and who would not believe her? In short, I am no friend to those who do things and chatter about it; I reject those who brag about things they haven't done; I am with those who want to and cannot. I don't love the ones who reveal secrets in the foulest way, or who talks about private things in the filthiest language. This is who I am, and I swear that there was never a suffering lover as faithful as me. Oh then, softest sweetest goddess, let me be the victor in this argument, in which I represent true love, and bless me with a sign of your great goodwill.

Here music is heard; doves are seen to flutter. They fall again upon their faces, then on their knees.

O thou that from eleven to ninety reign'st
In mortal bosoms, whose chase is this world,
And we in herds thy game, I give thee thanks
For this fair token, which being laid unto
Mine innocent true heart, arms in assurance
My body to this business.—Let us rise
And bow before the goddess. Time comes on.

Oh you who lives in the hearts of all men from eleven to ninety, whose hunting ground is this world, with us as your prey, I give you thanks for this sweet sign, which I will clasp to my true innocent heart, it gives my body confidence in this business.—Let us rise and bow to the goddess. It's almost time.

They bow. Exeunt.

Still music of records. Enter Emilia in white, her hair about her shoulders, and wearing a wheaten wreath; one in white holding up her train, her hair stuck with flowers; one before her carrying a silver hind, in which is convey'd incense and sweet odors, which being set upon the altar of Diana, her maids standing aloof, she sets fire to it; then they curtsy and kneel.

EMILIA

O sacred, shadowy, cold, and constant queen,
Abandoner of revels, mute, contemplative,
Sweet, solitary, white as chaste, and pure
As wind-fann'd snow, who to thy female knights
Allow'st no more blood than will make a blush,
Which is their order's robe: I here, thy priest,
Am humbled 'fore thine altar. O, vouchsafe,
With that thy rare green eye—which never yet
Beheld thing maculate—look on thy virgin,
And, sacred silver mistress, lend thine ear
(Which nev'r heard scurril term, into whose port
Ne'er ent'red wanton sound) to my petition,
Season'd with holy fear. This is my last
Of vestal office; I am bride-habited,
But maiden-hearted. A husband I have 'pointed,
But do not know him. Out of two I should
Choose one, and pray for his success, but I
Am guiltless of election. Of mine eyes
Were I to lose one, they are equal precious,
I could doom neither; that which perish'd should
Go to't unsentenc'd. Therefore, most modest queen,
He of the two pretenders that best loves me
And has the truest title in't, let him
Take off my wheaten garland, or else grant
The file and quality I hold I may
Continue in thy band.

O sacred, shadowy, cold and unchanging queen,
who leaves the dance, silent, thoughtful,
sweet, solitary, clean and white, and pure
as the driven snow, who allows your female knights
to have no more passion than blushing,
which is the dress of their order: I, your priest,
bows before your altar. Oh, grant my prayers,
look on your virgin with your beautiful green eye,
which has never looked on anything corrupt,
and, holy silver mistress, lend your ear
(which never heard any foul words
or disgusting sounds) to my plea,
which is touched with holy fear. This is my last
service as your virgin; I am dressed as a bride,
but have the heart of a virgin. I have chosen a husband,
but don't know who he is. Of the two I ought to
choose one, and pray for his success, but I
cannot make the choice. They are like my eyes,
the loss of either would be equally painful;
I can't condemn either of them; the one who dies
will not be sentenced to death by me. Therefore, most modest queen,
let the one who loves me best and
has the best rights to it, let him
become my husband, or otherwise grant that I
may keep my place amongst your virgins.

Here the hind vanishes under the altar, and in the place ascends a rose tree, having one rose upon it.

See what our general of ebbs and flows
Out from the bowels of her holy altar
With sacred act advances: but one rose!
If well inspir'd, this battle shall confound
Both these brave knights, and I, a virgin flow'r,
Must grow alone, unpluck'd.

*See what comes from our actions,
from the heart of her holy altar
a sacred thing appears: just one rose!
If I interpret this rightly, both these
brave knights will lose this battle, and I,
a virgin flower, must grow alone, unplucked.*

Here is heard a sudden twang of instruments, and the rose falls from the tree, which vanishes under the altar.

The flow'r is fall'n, the tree descends. O mistress,
Thou here dischargest me. I shall be gather'd,
I think so, but I know not thine own will:
Unclasp thy mystery.——I hope she's pleas'd,
Her signs were gracious.

The flower has fallen, the tree disappears.
O mistress, you're sending me away. I shall be married,
I think so, but I don't know what you plan:
reveal your mysteries—I hope she's pleased,
her signs seem to say so.

They curtsy and exeunt.

Scene II

A darkened room in the prison.

(Doctor, Jailer, Wooer, Daughter, Maid, First Messenger)

Enter Doctor, Jailer, and Wooer in habit of Palamon.

WOOER
No.

DOCTOR
Has this advice I told you done any good upon
her?

WOOER
O, very much; the maids that kept her company
Have half persuaded her that I am Palamon.
Within this half hour she came smiling to me,
And ask'd me what I would eat, and when I
would kiss her.
I told her, presently, and kiss'd her twice.

DOCTOR
'Twas well done. Twenty times had been far
better,
For there the cure lies mainly.

WOOER
Then she told me
She would watch with me tonight, for well she
knew
What hour my fit would take me.

DOCTOR
Let her do so,
And when your fit comes, fit her home, and
presently.

WOOER
She would have me sing.

DOCTOR
You did so?

Has this advice I gave you done any good?

Oh, very much; the girls who are with her
have got her halfway persuaded that I am
Palamon. Within the last half-hour she came to
me smiling and asked what I wanted to eat, and
when I would kiss her.
I told her, at once, and kissed her twice.

That's good. Twenty times would have been far
better,
for that's the main way she'll be cured.

Then she told me
she would sit up with me tonight, for she had a
good idea
of the time my desire would come upon me.

Let her do so,
and when it comes, share it with her, at once.

She wanted me to sing.

And did you?

No.

DOCTOR
'twas very ill done then.
You should observe her ev'ry way.

That wasn't good then.
You should follow her every whim.

WOOER
Alas,
I have no voice, sir, to confirm her that way.

Alas,
I cannot sing, sir, to please her in that way.

DOCTOR
That's all one, if ye make a noise.
If she entreat again, do any thing,
Lie with her, if she ask you.

That doesn't matter, as long as you make a
noise. If she asks you again, do anything,
sleep with her, if she asks you.

JAILER
Ho there, doctor!

Hang on now, doctor!

DOCTOR
Yes, in the way of cure.

It's all in the name of a cure.

JAILER
But first, by your leave,
I' th' way of honesty.

If you'll excuse me, we should think first
about the name of virginity.

DOCTOR
That's but a niceness.
Nev'r cast your child away for honesty.
Cure her first this way; then if she will be
honest,
She has the path before her.

That's just a detail.
Never reject your child for the sake of a word.
First cure her this way; then if she wants to be
honest,
she'll have the way in front of her.

JAILER
Thank ye, doctor.

Thank you, doctor.

DOCTOR
Pray bring her in
And let's see how she is.

Please bring her in
and let's see how she is.

JAILER
I will, and tell her
Her Palamon stays for her; but, doctor,
Methinks you are i' th' wrong still.

I will, and I'll tell her
her Palamon is waiting for her; but, doctor,
I still think you are wrong.

Exit Jailer.

DOCTOR
Go, go!

Go, go!

You fathers are fine fools. Her honesty!
And we should give her physic till we find
that—

WOOER
Why, do you think she is not honest, sir?

DOCTOR
How old is she?

WOOER
She's eighteen.

DOCTOR
She may be,
But that's all one, 'tis nothing to our purpose.
What e'er her father says, if you perceive
Her mood inclining that way that I spoke of,
Videlicet, the way of flesh—you have me?

WOOER
Yet very well, sir.

DOCTOR
Please her appetite,
And do it home; it cures her ipso facto
The melancholy humor that infects her.

WOOER
I am of your mind, doctor.

DOCTOR
You'll find it so. She comes. Pray humor her.

JAILER
Come, your love Palamon stays for you, child,
And has done this long hour, to visit you.

JAILER'S DAUGHTER
I thank him for his gentle patience,
He's a kind gentleman, and I am much bound
to him.
Did you nev'r see the horse he gave me?

You fathers are great fools. Her virginity!
Should we give her medicine until we find that–

What, do you think she's not a virgin, sir?

How old is she?

She's eighteen.

She may be a virgin,
it's all the same to me, it's nothing to do with
us. Whatever her father says, if you see
her mood starting to go in that direction,
I give you permission, enjoy her–you know
what I mean?

Very well, sir.

Satisfy her,
and do it well; it will cure her of this
depression of hers at once.

I agree with you, doctor.

Enter Jailer, Daughter, Maid.

You'll find I'm right. Here she comes. Please
humour her.

Wooer retires.

Come, your lover Palamon is waiting for you,
child, and has been for the past hour.

I thanked him for his kind patience,
he's a kind gentleman, and I'm devoted to him.
Did you not see the horse he gave me?

JAILER
Yes.

JAILER'S DAUGHTER
How do you like him?

JAILER
He's a very fair one.

JAILER'S DAUGHTER
You never saw him dance?

JAILER
No.

JAILER'S DAUGHTER
I have often.
He dances very finely, very comely,
And for a jig, come cut and long tail to him,
He turns ye like a top.

JAILER
That's fine indeed.

JAILER'S DAUGHTER
He'll dance the morris twenty mile an hour,
And that will founder the best hobby-horse
(If I have any skill) in all the parish,
And gallops to the tune of "Light a' love."
What think you of this horse?

JAILER
Having these virtues,
I think he might be brought to play at tennis.

JAILER'S DAUGHTER
Alas, that's nothing.

JAILER
Can he write and read too?

JAILER'S DAUGHTER
A very fair hand, and casts himself th' accounts
Of all his hay and provender. That hostler
Must rise betime that cozens him. You know
The chestnut mare the Duke has?

Yes.

What did you think of him?

He's a very good chap.

Did you never see him dance?

No.

I've seen him often.
He dances very finely, very gracefully,
and in a jig, come what may,
he spins you like a top.

That's wonderful.

He'll dance a Morris dance at twenty miles an
hour, and that will wear out the best
hobbyhorse (if I know anything about it) in the
whole parish,
and he gallops to the tune of "Light of love."
What do you think of this horse?

As he has all these accomplishments,
I think he should be brought to play tennis.

Alas, that's nothing.

Can he read and write too?

Very nicely, and he adds up all the accounts
for his hay and food. A stableman would have
to get up very early to cheat him. You know
the chestnut mare the Duke has?

JAILER
Very well.

Certainly.

JAILER'S DAUGHTER
She is horribly in love with him, poor beast,
But he is like his master, coy and scornful.

*She's massively in love with him, poor beast,
but he's like his master, standoffish and
scornful.*

JAILER
What dowry has she?

What dowry does she have?

JAILER'S DAUGHTER
Some two hundred bottles,
And twenty strike of oats, but he'll ne'er have
her.
He lisps in 's neighing able to entice
A miller's mare, he'll be the death of her.

*About two hundred bundles of hay,
and twenty bushels of oats, but he'll never have
her.
He has a lisp in his neigh that would attract
any mare, he'll be the death of her.*

DOCTOR
What stuff she utters!

What nonsense she talks!

JAILER
Make curtsy, here your love comes.

Curtsy, here comes you lover.

Wooer comes forward.

WOOER
Pretty soul,
How do ye? That's a fine maid! There's a
curtsy!

*Pretty soul,
how are you? There's a fine girl! What a
curtsy!*

JAILER'S DAUGHTER
Yours to command i' th' way of honesty.
How far is't now to th' end o' th' world, my
masters?

*I'm yours to command in an honest way.
How far is it to the end of the world, my
masters?*

DOCTOR
Why, a day's journey, wench.

Why, a day's journey, girl.

JAILER'S DAUGHTER
Will you go with me?

Will you go with me?

WOOER
What shall we do there, wench?

What shall we do there, girl?

JAILER'S DAUGHTER
Why, play at stoolball:

Why, play stoolball:

What is there else to do?

WOOER
I am content,
If we shall keep our wedding there.

JAILER'S DAUGHTER
'Tis true,
For there, I will assure you, we shall find
Some blind priest for the purpose that will venture
To marry us, for here they are nice and foolish.
Besides, my father must be hang'd tomorrow,
And that would be a blot i' th' business.
Are not you Palamon?

WOOER
Do not you know me?

JAILER'S DAUGHTER
Yes, but you care not for me. I have nothing
But this poor petticoat and two coarse smocks.

WOOER
That's all one, I will have you.

JAILER'S DAUGHTER
Will you surely?

WOOER
Yes, by this fair hand, will I.

JAILER'S DAUGHTER
We'll to bed then.

WOOER
Ev'n when you will.

JAILER'S DAUGHTER
O, sir, you would fain be nibbling.

WOOER
Why do you rub my kiss off?

what else is there to do?

I will be happy
if we get married there.

It's true,
I can promise you we shall find
some blind priest there who will agree
to marry us, for here they are fussy and foolish.
Besides, my father has to be hanged tomorrow,
and that would cast a shadow over the business.
Aren't you Palamon?

Don't you recognise me?

Yes, but you don't care about me. I own
nothing except this poor petticoat and two
rough dresses.

That doesn't matter, I'll take you.

Will you definitely?

Yes, by this lovely hand, I swear I will.

We'll go to bed then.

Whenever you like.

Kisses her.

Oh sir, you would like a nibble.

Why are you rubbing my kiss off?

JAILER'S DAUGHTER
'Tis a sweet one,
And will perfume me finely against the
wedding.
Is not this your cousin Arcite?

DOCTOR
Yes, sweet heart,
And I am glad my cousin Palamon
Has made so fair a choice.

JAILER'S DAUGHTER
Do you think he'll have me?

DOCTOR
Yes, without doubt.

JAILER'S DAUGHTER
Do you think so too?

JAILER
Yes.

JAILER'S DAUGHTER
We shall have many children.—Lord, how y'
are grown!
My Palamon I hope will grow too, finely,
Now he's at liberty. Alas, poor chicken,
He was kept down with hard meat and ill
lodging,
But I'll kiss him up again.

1. MESSENGER
What do you here? You'll lose the noblest sight
That ev'r was seen.

JAILER
Are they i' th' field?

1. MESSENGER
They are.
You bear a charge there too.

JAILER
I'll away straight.

It's a sweet one,
and it will do as perfume for the wedding.
Isn't this your cousin Arcite?

Yes, sweetheart,
and I am glad my cousin Palamon
has made such a good choice.

Do you think he'll have me?

Yes, no doubt.

Do you think so too?

Yes.

We shall have many children.-Lord, how you've
grown!
My Palamon and I will grow too, well,
now he's free. Alas, poor chick,
he was roughly treated with bad food and poor
rooms,
but I'll raise him up again with kisses.

Enter First Messenger.

What are you doing here? You'll miss the
noblest sight anyone's ever seen.

Are they on the battlefield?

They are.
You have a job there too.

I'll come at once.

I must ev'n leave you here.

DOCTOR
Nay, we'll go with you,
I will not lose the fight.

JAILER
How did you like her?

DOCTOR
I'll warrant you within these three or four days
I'll make her right again.

You must not from her,
But still preserve her in this way.

WOOER
I will.

DOCTOR
Let's get her in.

WOOER
Come, sweet, we'll go to dinner,
And then we'll play at cards.

JAILER'S DAUGHTER
And shall we kiss too?

WOOER
A hundred times.

JAILER'S DAUGHTER
And twenty?

WOOER
Ay, and twenty.

JAILER'S DAUGHTER
And then we'll sleep together?

DOCTOR
Take her offer.

I must leave you here.

No, we'll go with you,
I don't want to miss the fight.

What did you think of her?

I promise you that within the next three or four
days I'll get her right again.

To the Wooer.

You mustn't leave her,
but keep this pretence up.

I will.

Let's get her inside.

Come, sweet, we'll go into dinner,
and then we'll play cards.

And shall we kiss too?

A hundred times.

And twenty?

Yes, and twenty.

And then we'll sleep together?

Accept her offer.

WOOER
Yes, marry, will we.

JAILER'S DAUGHTER
But you shall not hurt me.

WOOER
I will not, sweet.

JAILER'S DAUGHTER
If you do, love, I'll cry.

Yes, we certainly will.

But you won't hurt me.

I won't, sweetheart.

If you do, love, I'll cry

Exeunt.

Scene III

A place near the Lists.

(Theseus, Hippolyta, Emilia, Pirithous, Attendants, Servants, Arcite)

Flourish. Enter Theseus, Hippolyta, Emilia, Pirithous, and some Attendants.

EMILIA
I'll no step further.

PIRITHOUS
Will you lose this sight?

EMILIA
I had rather see a wren hawk at a fly
Than this decision. Ev'ry blow that falls
Threats a brave life, each stroke laments
The place whereon it falls, and sounds more
like
A bell than blade. I will stay here,
It is enough my hearing shall be punish'd
With what shall happen—'gainst the which
there is
No deafing—but to hear, not taint mine eye
With dread sights it may shun.

PIRITHOUS
Sir, my good lord,
Your sister will no further.

THESEUS
O, she must.
She shall see deeds of honor in their kind
Which sometime show well, pencill'd. Nature
now
Shall make and act the story, the belief
Both seal'd with eye and ear. You must be
present,
You are the victor's meed, the price and
garland
To crown the question's title.

EMILIA

I'll go no further.

Do you want to miss the fight?

I'd sooner see a wren attacking a fly
than this battle. Every blow that falls
threatens a brave life, every stroke causes
sorrow as it falls, and sounds more like
a funeral bell than a blade. I will stay here,
it's bad enough that I will suffer hearing
what will happen-nothing can make me deaf
to that-I'll just hear, not stain my vision
which such terrible sights, when they can be
avoided.

Sir, my good lord,
your sister wants to stop here.

Oh, she must come on.
She shall see such deeds of honour that will
later make a fine painting. You shall see the
story
created by Nature, and you need to use
your eyes and ears for that. You must be there,
you are the winner's prize, the reward and
trophy
when the question is resolved.

Pardon me,
If I were there, I'ld wink.

THESEUS
You must be there;
This trial is as 'twere i' th' night, and you
The only star to shine.

EMILIA
I am extinct,
There is but envy in that light which shows
The one the other. Darkness, which ever was
The dam of Horror, who does stand accurs'd
Of many mortal millions, may even now,
By casting her black mantle over both,
That neither could find other, get herself
Some part of a good name, and many a murder
Set off whereto she's guilty.

HIPPOLYTA
You must go.

EMILIA
In faith, I will not.

THESEUS
Why, the knights must kindle
Their valor at your eye. Know, of this war
You are the treasure, and must needs be by
To give the service pay.

EMILIA
Sir, pardon me,
The title of a kingdom may be tried
Out of itself.

THESEUS
Well, well then, at your pleasure.
Those that remain with you could wish their office
To any of their enemies.

HIPPOLYTA
Farewell, sister,
I am like to know your husband 'fore yourself
By some small start of time. He whom the gods

Excuse me,
If I was there, I would faint.

You must be there,
it's as if this trail were at night time, and you
are the only star shining.

I am dark to them,
it's only hatred which lets them see
each other. Darkness, which has always
created horror, which is hated
by so many millions of men, could now,
by throwing her black cloak over both,
so that neither could find the other, get herself
something of a good name, and be forgiven
many of the murders she's been responsible for.

You must go.

I swear I won't.

Why, the knights need to get
their bravery from your looks. You are the
treasure they're fighting for, and you must
be on hand to pay the bill.

Sir, excuse me,
people can fight for a kingdom
outside its borders.

Well, well then, as you wish.
Those who stay with you will wish
their enemies were in their place.

Farewell, sister.
It seems I will know who your husband is
a little while before you do. I pray that

Do of the two know best, I pray them he
Be made your lot.

EMILIA
Arcite is gently visag'd; yet his eye
Is like an engine bent, or a sharp weapon
In a soft sheath; mercy and manly courage
Are bedfellows in his visage. Palamon
Has a most menacing aspect, his brow
Is grav'd, and seems to bury what it frowns on,
Yet sometime 'tis not so, but alters to
The quality of his thoughts; long time his eye
Will dwell upon his object; melancholy
Becomes him nobly. So does Arcite's mirth,
But Palamon's sadness is a kind of mirth,
So mingled as if mirth did make him sad,
And sadness merry; those darker humors that
Stick misbecomingly on others, on him
Live in fair dwelling.

Hark how yon spurs to spirit do incite
The princes to their proof! Arcite may win me,
And yet may Palamon wound Arcite to
The spoiling of his figure. O, what pity
Enough for such a chance? If I were by,
I might do hurt, for they would glance their
eyes
Toward my seat, and in that motion might
Omit a ward, or forfeit an offense,
Which crav'd that very time. It is much better
I am not there. O, better never born
Than minister to such harm!

What is the chance?

SERV.
The cry's "A Palamon!"

*you get the one who is most favoured
by the gods.*

Exeunt Theseus, Hippolyta, Pirithous, etc.

*Arcite has a sweet face, but his eye
is like a coiled spring, or a sharp weapon
in a soft sheath; mercy and manly courage
share his face. Palamon
looks very fierce, his brow
is furrowed, and it seems to want to kill what it
frowns at, but sometimes it isn't, but changes
depending on his thoughts; he will
gaze on his subject for a long time,
sorrow suits him well. So does Arcite's
laughter, but Palamon's sadness is a kind of
laughter, he's so mixed it's as if laughter makes
him sad, and sadness happy; those dark moods
that look so unpleasant in others
look sweet on him.*

Cornets. Trumpets sound as to a charge.

*Hear how those spirit lifting sounds call
the princes to their test! Arcite might win me,
but Palamon might wound Arcite in such a way
as to spoil his looks. That would be an
impossibly pitiful outcome. If I were near,
I might do harm, because they would glance
towards me, and as they did they might
miss a chance to defend or attack
that was theirs for the taking. It is much better
that I am not there. Oh, it would have been
better for me never to be born rather than be
the the cause of such harm!*

Cornets. A great cry and noise within, crying

"A Palamon!"

Enter Servant.

What's happened?

They're shouting, "For Palamon!"

154

EMILIA
Then he has won. 'Twas ever likely:
He look'd all grace and success, and he is
Doubtless the prim'st of men. I prithee run
And tell me how it goes.

Then he has won. It was always likely:
he looked the most graceful and victorious,
and he is surely the greatest of men. Please run
and tell me what's happened.

Shout and cornets. Crying "A Palamon!" within.

SERV.
Still "Palamon!"

Still "Palamon!"

EMILIA
Run and inquire.

Run and ask.

Exit Servant.

Poor servant, thou hast lost.
Upon my right side still I wore thy picture,
Palamon's on the left. Why so, I know not;
I had no end in't else; chance would have it so.
On the sinister side the heart lies; Palamon
Had the best-boding chance.

Poor servant, you have lost.
I carried your picture on my right side,
with Palamon's on the left. Why I did, I don't
know; I had no other hand in it; that's how fate
decreed. The heart is on the left side; Palamon
had the best chance.

Another cry, and shout within, and cornets.

This burst of clamor
Is sure th' end o' th' combat.

This outburst
surely marks the end of the fight.

Enter Servant.

SERV.
They said that Palamon had Arcite's body
Within an inch o' th' pyramid, that the cry
Was general "A Palamon!"; but anon
Th' assistants made a brave redemption, and
The two bold titlers at this instant are
Hand to hand at it.

They said that Palamon had Arcite's body
within an inch of the pyramid, and the cry went
up, "Palamon's won!"; but quickly
his seconds saved him, and
the two bold combatants are still
at it, hand to hand.

EMILIA
Were they metamorphis'd
Both into one—O why? There were no woman
Worth so compos'd a man! Their single share,
Their nobleness peculiar to them, gives
The prejudice of disparity, value's shortness,
To any lady breathing.

I wish they could both be made into one man-
Why wish that? There's no woman
who deserves a man like that! Their individual
qualities, the nobility that's all their own,
already make them far above the value
of any lady alive.

More exulting?

More cheering?

Cornets. Cry within, "Arcite, Arcite!"

"Palamon" still?

Still "Palamon"?

SERV.
Nay, now the sound is "Arcite."

No, now they're calling "Arcite".

EMILIA
I prithee lay attention to the cry;
Set both thine ears to th' business.

*Please pay attention to what they're calling;
listen as carefully as you can.*

Cornets. A great shout and cry, "Arcite! Victory!"

SERV.
The cry is
"Arcite!" and "victory!" Hark, "Arcite!
Victory!"
The combat's consummation is proclaim'd
By the wind instruments.

*They're calling
"Arcite!" and "victory!" Listen, "Arcite!
Victory!"
The end of the fight is marked
by the trumpets.*

EMILIA
Half-sights saw
That Arcite was no babe. God's lid, his richness
And costliness of spirit look'd through him, it could
No more be hid in him than fire in flax,
Than humble banks can go to law with waters
That drift-winds force to raging. I did think
Good Palamon would miscarry, yet I knew not
Why I did think so. Our reasons are not prophets
When oft our fancies are. They are coming off.
Alas, poor Palamon!

*Half blind people could see
that Arcite was no child. I swear, his strength
and wonderful spirit were obvious, it couldn't
be hidden any more than fire in flax,
any more than low banks can keep back the sea
when the storm winds whip it into fury. I thought
good Palamon would lose, but I don't know why
I thought so. We often can't logically predict
things our imaginations know. They are
coming away.
Alas, poor Palamon!*

Cornets.

Enter Theseus, Hippolyta, Pirithous, Arcite as victor, and Attendants, etc.

THESEUS
Lo, where our sister is in expectation,
Yet quaking and unsettled. Fairest Emily,
The gods by their divine arbitrement
Have given you this knight: he is a good one
As ever strook at head. Give me your hands.
Receive you her, you him, be plighted with
A love that grows as you decay.

*See where my sister waits expectantly,
but shaking and worried. Fairest Emily,
the gods have by divine judgment
given you this knight: he is as good a man
as ever struck a blow. Give me your hands.
You take her, you take him, be joined with
a love that grows as you get older.*

ARCITE

Emily,
To buy you I have lost what's dearest to me
Save what is bought, and yet I purchase cheaply,
As I do rate your value.

THESEUS

O loved sister,
He speaks now of as brave a knight as e'er
Did spur a noble steed. Surely the gods
Would have him die a bachelor, lest his race
Should show i' th' world too godlike. His behavior
So charm'd me that methought Alcides was
To him a sow of lead. If I could praise
Each part of him to th' all I have spoke, your Arcite
Did not lose by't; for he that was thus good
Encount'red yet his better. I have heard
Two emulous Philomels beat the ear o' th' night
With their contentious throats, now one the higher,
Anon the other, then again the first,
And by and by out-breasted, that the sense
Could not be judge between 'em. So it far'd
Good space between these kinsmen; till heavens did
Make hardly one the winner.—Wear the girlond
With joy that you have won.—For the subdu'd,
Give them our present justice, since I know
Their lives but pinch 'em. Let it here be done.
The scene's not for our seeing, go we hence,
Right joyful, with some sorrow.—Arm your prize,
I know you will not loose her.—Hippolyta,
I see one eye of yours conceives a tear,
The which it will deliver.

EMILIA

Is this winning?
O all you heavenly powers, where is your mercy?
But that your wills have said it must be so,

Emily,
to buy you I have lost what was dearest to me
apart from what I bought, but the price I put on you
makes you a bargain at the price.

Oh beloved sister,
he's talking about as brave a knight who ever
rode a good horse. Surely the gods
wanted him to die a bachelor, in case he should bring
children into the world who were too like gods. I found
his behaviour so charming that I thought Alcides
was a block of lead in comparison. If I could praise
every part of him in this way, your Arcite
wouldn't lose by the comparison; he that was so good
came across his better. I have heard
two battling nightingales singing their
competing songs in the night, one louder
then the other, then the first again,
then the second, until one
couldn't judge between them. It was like this
for a long time between these kinsmen; until the
heavens just allowed one to edge it. Wear the
garland you have won with joy. For the losers,
execute my sentence on them at once, for I
know their lives are now painful to them. Let it
be done here.
We don't want to see it, let's leave,
very happy but with some sorrow. - Take your prize,
I know you won't let her go.- Hippolyta,
I can see there is a tear in your eye,
about to fall.

Is this victory?
Oh all you gods, where is your mercy?
If it wasn't for the fact that you have decreed it,
and ordered me to live to make happy this

And charge me live to comfort this unfriended,
This miserable prince, that cuts away
A life more worthy from him than all women,
I should and would die too.

HIPPOLYTA
Infinite pity
That four such eyes should be so fix'd on one
That two must needs be blind for't!

THESEUS
So it is.

friendless
miserable prince, who has taken from himself
a life more worthy than all woman combined,
I would wish to die as well.

It's a horrible shame
that four eyes like these should have chosen to
look at one woman, so that two of them had to
be blinded to settle it!

Indeed it is.

Flourish. Exeunt

Scene IV

A place near the Lists. A block prepared.

(Palamon, Three Knights, Jailer, Executioner, Guard, Second Messenger, Pirithous, Theseus, Hippolyta, Emilia, Arcite)

A block ready. Enter Palamon and his Knights pinion'd, Jailer, Executioner, etc., Guard.

PALAMON
There's many a man alive that hath outliv'd
The love o' th' people, yea, i' th' self-same state
Stands many a father with his child. Some comfort
We have by so considering: we expire,
And not without men's pity; to live still,
Have their good wishes; we prevent
The loathsome misery of age, beguile
The gout and rheum, that in lag hours attend
For grey approachers; we come towards the gods
Young and unwapper'd, not halting under crimes
Many and stale. That sure shall please the gods
Sooner than such, to give us nectar with 'em,
For we are more clear spirits. My dear kinsmen,
Whose lives (for this poor comfort) are laid down,
You have sold 'em too too cheap.

FIRST KNIGHT
What ending could be
Of more content? O'er us the victors have
Fortune, whose title is as momentary
As to us death is certain. A grain of honor
They not o'erweigh us.

SECOND KNIGHT
Let us bid farewell;
And with our patience anger tott'ring Fortune,
Who at her certain'st reels.

THIRD KNIGHT

159

There are many men alive who have outlived
the love of the people, and many fathers
outlive the love of their children. This is
a comforting thought: we are dying
with men pitying us; if we lived,
we should have their good wishes; we're
avoiding
the horrible misery of growing old, cheat the
gout and rheumatism that attack greybeards
in later life; we approach the gods
young and still fresh, not limping under the
burden
of numerous ancient crimes. The gods are
bound to
prefer us to that type, to let us drink nectar with
them,
for we are the purer spirits. My dear kinsmen,
whose lives are being sacrificed for this poor
comfort,
you have sold them far too cheap.

What happier ending could
we have? The ones who triumphed over us
had luck, which is as ephemeral as
our death is certain. They do not outweigh us
in honour by an ounce.

Let us say goodbye;
and let our stoicism anger wavering fortune,
who is shaky at her firmest.

Come! Who begins?

Come! Who shall go first?

PALAMON
Ev'n he that led you to this banquet shall
Taste to you all.
To the Jailer.
Ah ha, my friend, my friend,
Your gentle daughter gave me freedom once;
You'll see't done now forever. Pray how does she?
I heard she was not well; her kind of ill
Gave me some sorrow.

The one who brought you to this banquet shall taste the food for you all.
[To the jailer]
Aha, my friend, my friend,
your sweet daughter gave me my freedom once; now you'll give it to me for eternity. Tell me, how is she?
I heard she was not well; for her to be ill made me sad.

JAILER
Sir, she's well restor'd,
And to be married shortly.

Sir, she's back in good health, and will be married shortly.

PALAMON
By my short life,
I am most glad on't. 'Tis the latest thing
I shall be glad of, prithee tell her so.
Commend me to her, and to piece her portion
Tender her this.

I swear by my short life, that makes me very happy. It's the last thing I shall be happy about, please tell her so. Remember me to her, and give her this as a dowry.

Gives purse.

FIRST KNIGHT
Nay, let's be offerers all.

Let's all put in for this.

SECOND KNIGHT
Is it a maid?

Is she a good girl?

PALAMON
Verily I think so,
A right good creature, more to me deserving
Than I can quite or speak of.

I certainly think so, a very fine creature, whom I owe more than I can repay or describe.

ALL THREE KNIGHTS
Commend us to her.

Remember us to her.

They give their purses.

JAILER
The gods requite you all, and make her thankful!

May the gods repay you all, and make her grateful!

PALAMON
Adieu; and let my life be now as short

Goodbye; and now let my life be as short

As my leave-taking.

as the time it takes to leave.

Lies on the block.

THIRD KNIGHT
Lead, courageous cousin.

Lead on, brave cousin.

BOTH FIRST KNIGHT AND SECOND KNIGHT
We'll follow cheerfully.

We shall gladly follow.

A great noise within crying "Run! Save! Hold!"

Enter in haste a Messenger.

2. MESSENGER
Hold, hold! O, hold, hold, hold!

Wait, wait! Oh, wait, wait, wait!

Enter Pirithous in haste.

PIRITHOUS
Hold ho! It is a cursed haste you made
If you have done so quickly. Noble Palamon,
The gods will show their glory in a life
That thou art yet to lead.

*Wait there! Your haste will be cursed
if you finish the job so quickly. Noble Palamon,
the gods will show their glory in
your future life.*

PALAMON
Can that be, when
Venus I have said is false? How do things fare?

*How can that be, when
what Venus has said is false? What's going on?*

PIRITHOUS
Arise, great sir, and give the tidings ear

That are most dearly sweet and bitter.

Arise, great Sir, and listen to the news
Palamon rises.
that is both wonderful and bitter.

PALAMON
What
Hath wak'd us from our dream?

*What
has woken us from our dream?*

PIRITHOUS
List then: your cousin,
Mounted upon a steed that Emily
Did first bestow on him—a black one, owing
Not a hair-worth of white, which some will say
Weakens his price, and many will not buy
His goodness with this note; which superstition
Here finds allowance—on this horse is Arcite
Trotting the stones of Athens, which the calkins
Did rather tell than trample; for the horse

*Listen then: your cousin,
riding a horse that Emily
had given him–a black one, without
a single white hair, which some would say
makes it less valuable, and many wouldn't
accept his goodness because of it; this
superstition is confirmed by this–on this horse
Arcite was riding through Athens, its hooves
just touching stones rather than trampling*

Would make his length a mile, if't pleas'd his rider
To put pride in him. As he thus went counting
The flinty pavement, dancing as 'twere to th'
music
His own hoofs made (for as they say from iron
Came music's origin), what envious flint,
Cold as old Saturn, and like him possess'd
With fire malevolent, darted a spark,
Or what fierce sulphur else, to this end made,
I comment not—the hot horse, hot as fire,
Took toy at this, and fell to what disorder
His power could give his will, bounds, comes on end,
Forgets school-doing, being therein train'd,
And of kind manage; pig-like he whines
At the sharp rowel, which he frets at rather
Than any jot obeys; seeks all foul means
Of boist'rous and rough jad'ry, to disseat
His lord that kept it bravely. When nought serv'd,
When neither curb would crack, girth break, nor diff'ring plunges
Disroot his rider whence he grew, but that
He kept him 'tween his legs, on his hind hoofs
On end he stands,
That Arcite's legs, being higher than his head,
Seem'd with strange art to hang. His victor's wreath
Even then fell off his head; and presently
Backward the jade comes o'er, and his full poise
Becomes the rider's load. Yet is he living,
But such a vessel 'tis that floats but for
The surge that next approaches. He much desires
To have some speech with you. Lo he appears.

PALAMON
O miserable end of our alliance!
The gods are mighty, Arcite. If thy heart,
Thy worthy, manly heart, be yet unbroken,
Give me thy last words; I am Palamon,
One that yet loves thee dying.

them, for the horse could stride a mile in a pace, if his rider was prepared
to put trust in him. As he went forward over the stony pavement, as if he were dancing to the music
his own hooves made (for they say that music originates in iron), some malevolent flint,
as cold as old Saturn, and like him filled with evil fire, made a spark,
or some other piece of hellfire caused it,
I can't say–the passionate horse, passionate as fire, shied at this, and became as out-of-control
as his power would allow, leaping, bucking, forgetting his schooling, as he had been trained, becoming unmanageable; he whined like a pig at the feel of the spurs, which made him worse rather than making him obey; he tried all the dirty ways
of rowdy and rough horses, to throw off his lord, who stuck bravely to the saddle. When nothing worked,
when the bit wouldn't crack, the girth break, and the
different leaps couldn't throw off his rider, who still stayed in the saddle, he stood up on his hind hoofs,
so that Arcite's legs, being higher than his head,
seemed to hang as if by magic. His victor's wreath
fell off his head; and at once the horse fell over backwards, and his full weight
landed on the rider. He is still alive, but only like a ship that still floats until the next wave comes. He very much wants to talk with you. Look, here he comes.

Enter Theseus, Hippolyta, Emilia, Arcite in a chair.

What a miserable end to our friendship!
The gods are mighty, Arcite. If your heart,
your worthy, manly heart, be still working,
give me your last words; I am Palamon,
one who loves you still even in death.

ARCITE
Take Emilia,
And with her all the world's joy. Reach thy hand;
Farewell. I have told my last hour; I was false,
Yet never treacherous. Forgive me, cousin.
One kiss from fair Emilia.—'Tis done.
Take her. I die.

PALAMON
Thy brave soul seek Elysium!

EMILIA
I'll close thine eyes, prince; blessed souls be
with thee!
Thou art a right good man, and while I live,
This day I give to tears.

PALAMON
And I to honor.

THESEUS
In this place first you fought; ev'n very here
I sund'red you. Acknowledge to the gods
Our thanks that you are living.
His part is play'd, and though it were too short,
He did it well; your day is length'ned, and
The blissful dew of heaven does arrouse you.
The powerful Venus well hath grac'd her altar,
And given you your love. Our master Mars
Hath vouch'd his oracle, and to Arcite gave
The grace of the contention So the deities
Have show'd due justice.—Bear this hence.

PALAMON
O cousin,
That we should things desire which do cost us
The loss of our desire! That nought could buy
Dear love but loss of dear love!

THESEUS
Never fortune
Did play a subtler game. The conquer'd
triumphs,

Take Emilia,
and with her all the happiness in the world.
Give me your hand;
Farewell. I have seen my last hour; I was
wrong, but never treacherous. Forgive me,
cousin. One kiss from lovely Emilia.—It's done.
Take her. I'm dying.

Dies.

May your brave soul find Elysium!

I'll close your eyes, prince; may you go to the
blessed souls!
You are truly a good man, and for my whole life
I will commemorate this day with tears.

And I with honour.

This is where you first fought; the very place
where I parted you. Give the gods
thanks that you are alive.
He's played his part, and though it was too
short, he did it well; your time has been
extended, and the blessed dew of heaven falls
on you. Powerful Venus has shone her light on
her altar and given you your love. Our master
Mars has fulfilled his promise, and given Arcite
the victory. So the gods
have shown fair justice.—Carry this away.

Arcite is carried out.

O cousin,
why did we have to desire things which cost us
things we desired! Why could nothing buy
dear love except for losing dear love!

Fate never
played a more cunning game. The loser wins,
the winner loses; but the gods have still been

164

The victor has the loss; yet in the passage
The gods have been most equal. Palamon,
Your kinsman hath confess'd the right o' th'
lady
Did lie in you, for you first saw her, and
Even then proclaim'd your fancy. He restor'd
her
As your stol'n jewel, and desir'd your spirit
To send him hence forgiven. The gods my
justice
Take from my hand, and they themselves
become
The executioners. Lead your lady off;
And call your lovers from the stage of death,
Whom I adopt my friends. A day or two
Let us look sadly, and give grace unto
The funeral of Arcite, in whose end
The visages of bridegrooms we'll put on
And smile with Palamon; for whom an hour,
But one hour since, I was as dearly sorry
As glad of Arcite; and am now as glad
As for him sorry. O you heavenly charmers,
What things you make of us! For what we lack
We laugh, for what we have are sorry, still
Are children in some kind. Let us be thankful
For that which is, and with you leave dispute
That are above our question. Let's go off,
And bear us like the time.

perfectly fair. Palamon,
your kinsman admitted that you had
the rights to the lady, for you saw her first, and
declared your love at the time. He gave her
back to you as your stolen jewel, and asked you
to send him away forgiven. The gods have taken
my powers of justice out of my hand, and they
have become
the executioners themselves. Take your lady
away;
and call your followers off the scaffold,
they are now my friends. Let us mourn
for a day or two, and honour the
funeral of Arcite, and at the end of that
we'll assume the faces of bridegrooms
and smile with Palamon; for whom
just an hour ago I was as sorry to have lost
as I was glad to have Arcite; and now I am as
glad
to have him as I am sorry for Arcite. Oh you
gods,
what things you make of us! We love things
we don't have, don't like what we have, we're
still
like children in some ways. Let us be thankful
for the way things are, and leave you to decide
things that are beyond us. Let us go,
and make the most of our time.

Flourish. Exeunt.

(Epilogue)

EPILOGUE

I would now ask ye how ye like the play,
But as it is with schoolboys, cannot say;
I am cruel fearful. Pray yet stay a while,
And let me look upon ye. No man smile?
Then it goes hard, I see. He that has
Lov'd a young handsome wench then, show his
face—
'Tis strange if none be here—and if he will
Against his conscience, let him hiss, and kill
Our market. 'Tis in vain, I see, to stay ye;
Have at the worst can come, then! Now what
say ye?
And yet mistake me not: I am not bold,

I would ask you now how you like the play,
but I'm like a schoolboy, I can't ask;
I am very afraid. Please stay awhile,
and let me look at you. Is nobody smiling?
Then you don't like it, I see. If anyone here
has loved a handsome young girl, show his
face—
it would be strange if there were none—and if he
wants to be a hypocrite, let him hiss, and ruin
our ticket sales. I can see there's no point in
trying to stop you;
give it your worst then! Now what do you say?
And yet don't misunderstand me: I am not

We have no such cause. If the tale we have told
(For 'tis no other) any way content ye
(For to that honest purpose it was meant ye),
We have our end; and ye shall have ere long
I dare say many a better, to prolong
Your old loves to us. We, and all our might,
Rest at your service. Gentlemen, good night.

angry, we have no reason to be. If the story we have told (for it's just a story) has pleased you in any way (for that was what we were trying to do), we have our reward; and I daresay before long you will see many better plays, and that will make you remain as our patrons. We, and all our strength,
are at your service. Gentlemen, good night.

Flourish.

Made in the USA
Middletown, DE
19 July 2019